Beth

Love, Skip, Jump

love,

Shelene Bryan

PRAISE FOR *LOVE, SKIP, JUMP*

"Shelene is one of those people whose joy is contagious. She leaks Jesus. In the pages of *Love, Skip, Jump* she invites you not to sit down for coffee and talk about your faith, but to break down the doors and start doing something. This is a book you'll want to read, but not keep to yourself. It's a message we all need to hear."

—BOB GOFF, *NEW YORK TIMES* BEST-SELLING AUTHOR OF *LOVE DOES*

"Shelene Bryan is passionate, she's caring and she's having the time of her life helping other people realize that they can matter too."

—SETH GODIN, AUTHOR OF *THE ICARUS DECEPTION*

"This book is life-changing. Run. Skip. Jump. Whatever you have to do to get a copy. This book will change your life and open your eyes. Shelene Bryan has always been my friend. Now she's one of my favorite authors."

—#1 *NEW YORK TIMES* BEST-SELLING NOVELIST
KAREN KINGSBURY, AUTHOR OF *FIFTEEN MINUTES*

"If *Love, Skip, Jump* doesn't push you out of your comfort zone in the best possible way, I don't know what will."

—CANDACE CAMERON BURE, ACTRESS, AUTHOR, PRODUCER

"Shelene is able to take people on a positive journey through her world-changing ideas . . . it's cool to be comfortable with being uncomfortable."

—DREW RYNIEWICZ, SINGER-SONGWRITER

"Shelene Bryan is a brilliant, one of a kind storyteller. I was first introduced to Shelene through her TEDx talk that inspired our nation. I cheered, clapped my hands, and then pressed replay the moment my husband walked through the door. Take that excitement, multiply it by 100, and that's how you will feel reading *Love, Skip, Jump*. Shelene makes a case for saying no to ourselves and yes to a life that consistently and continuously says yes to God. You'll quickly realize, you'd be crazy not to say yes!"

—FAWN WEAVER, *NEW YORK TIMES* BEST-
SELLING AUTHOR OF *HAPPY WIVES CLUB*

"This book is a breath of fresh air! *Love, Skip, Jump* packs a *powerful* punch that will knock the 'couch potato, me-centered Christianity' right out of you. If you truly want to live a God inspired life filled with adventure, purpose, and meaning then this book is definitely for you."

—BYRON DAVIS, FORMER AMERICAN RECORD HOLDER,
AUTHOR, AND FOUNDER OF EPICLIFEPROJECT.COM

"If anyone can get you to say yes, it is Shelene Bryan. This book may change your life. I dare you to read the book . . . I dare you to live the full life God wants you to have here on earth."

—SHANNON MCINTOSH, MOM, WIFE, PRODUCER

"Shelene's personal journey challenges us to 'jump in' with our Creator, and make our lives count."

—BOB BRADBERRY, PASTOR OF SADDLEBACK CHURCH,
PEACE PLAN GLOBAL FIELD COORDINATION

"*Love, Skip, Jump* is a challenging book that will warm your heart. If you are looking for a good read, this is the book for you. If you are overwhelmed with questions about God, who He is, and what His plan is for you, this book is for you."

—ASHLEY SMITH ROBINSON, AUTHOR OF *UNLIKELY ANGEL*

Love, Skip, Jump

START LIVING THE ADVENTURE OF *YES*

SHELENE BRYAN

NELSON
BOOKS

An Imprint of Thomas Nelson

Published in Nashville, Tennessee, by Nelson Books, an imprint of Thomas Nelson. Nelson Books and Thomas Nelson are registered trademarks of HarperCollins Christian Publishing, Inc.

Author is represented by the literary agency of Alive Communications, Inc., 7680 Goddard Street, Suite 200, Colorado Springs, Colorado 80920, www .alivecommunications.com.

Thomas Nelson titles may be purchased in bulk for educational, business, fund-raising, or sales promotional use. For information, please e-mail SpecialMarkets@ThomasNelson.com.

Unless otherwise indicated, Scripture quotations are taken from the Holy Bible, New International Version®, NIV®. Copyright © 1973, 1978, 1984, 2011 by Biblica, Inc.™ Used by permission of Zondervan. All rights reserved worldwide. www.zondervan.com

Scripture quotations marked MSG are taken from *The Message* by Eugene H. Peterson. © 1993, 1994, 1995, 1996, 2000. Used by permission of NavPress Publishing Group. All rights reserved.

The Library of Congress Cataloging-in-Publication Data
is on file with the Library of Congress.

ISBN 978-1-4002-0616-2

Printed in the United States of America

14 15 16 17 18 19 RRD 6 5 4 3 2 1

To God Almighty, the giver of everything. Thank You for always being the hero of the story.

To you, the reader:
I thought about you while I was writing every chapter of this book. I know that we have most likely never met and I don't even know your name, but that didn't stop me from praying that this book would set you on an adventure of a lifetime. Thank you for purchasing this book and helping us build kitchens all over the world to feed children and families in need. Contact me anytime to share your Love, Skip, Jump adventures. I'd love to hear from you at Shelenebryan.com.

Contents

CONTENTS

foreword

If you had told me twenty years ago that I was going to write a foreword for Shelene Bryan's book about saying yes to God, I would have thought you were crazy. She was loud, materialistic, self-centered . . . you get the picture. Little did I know that God was going to transform her into a humble, generous, and godly woman. She is still pretty loud but about things that matter. Brice and Shelene are dear friends of ours. Lisa and I love ministering with them and look forward to an eternity of laughter and friendship.

Few things annoy me more than "Christians" who listen to sermons, memorize verses, and do nothing. That's why it was a joy to be Shelene's pastor for fifteen years. She was a "doer of the Word and not merely a hearer" as James 1 describes. While others were discussing and critiquing sermons, I could count on Shelene to actually do something. I watched her heart break during her first trip to Africa, and I got excited because I knew that actions would follow.

> Let us not love with words or speech but with actions and in truth. (1 John 3:18)

I read *Love, Skip, Jump* in one sitting. I could not put it down! I loved many things about this book, but what I loved most is the tone. I found myself smiling and laughing my way through it. And that's the way it should be. Caring for others should be less about guilt and obligation and more about love and joy! Following the footsteps of Jesus is painful at times, but obedience leads to life.

God loves a cheerful giver. (2 Corinthians 9:7)

They are to do good, to be rich in good works, to be generous and ready to share, thus storing up treasure for themselves as a good foundation for the future, so that they may take hold of that which is truly life. (1 Timothy 6:18–19)

Don't miss that last phrase: *"that they may take hold of that which is truly life."* Have you taken hold of it? Do you wake up with eagerness? I meet so many people who don't have that light in their eyes. They have moments of pleasure but they know something is still missing. They grasp for the next thing that will make them happy. They don't realize that true life comes from letting go.

For whoever would save his life will lose it, but whoever loses his life for my sake will find it. (Matthew 16:25)

Don't be another person who wastes his/her life by trying to save it. Spend more energy saving lives than saving for retirement. Just consider the possibility that you might live more if you risked more and gave more. Join my friend Shelene in doing something. You will make mistakes (I've watched her make plenty), but you are guaranteed to make mistakes by doing nothing.

There is so much joy in rescuing people from their afflictions. You will miss out on life by ignoring them. My fondest memories are the times I fought for others. Those are times of tears, laughs, victories, and failures. Those are times of living real adventure. Don't waste another day. Love, skip, jump, or at least take a step. Real people with real needs are waiting for you.

Francis Chan

Introduction

In the cherished children's classic *Willy Wonka & the Chocolate Factory*[1] (1971 musical), the lovable Charlie Bucket finds a Golden Ticket in a Wonka Bar and wins the opportunity, along with four other children, to tour the zaniest, most wonderful candy factory in the world with his favorite person, Grandpa Joe. One of my favorite scenes in this iconic film is when Willy Wonka is escorting the group of winners down a colorful hallway inside the factory. As Wonka passes a wall adorned with fruit-striped wallpaper, he abruptly stops. With a huge grin and an obvious swell of pride, he says, "Wait a minute. Must show you this. Lickable wallpaper for nursery walls. Lick an orange, it tastes like an orange. Lick a pineapple, it taste like a pineapple. Go ahead, try it."

Kids and adults alike begin licking the fruit portrayed on the wallpaper in earnest.

"Mm, I got a plum," says one kid.

"This banana's fantastic!" Charlie exclaims. "It tastes so real."

Wonka urges them on. "Try some more. Strawberries taste like strawberries. The shnozberries taste like shnozberries!"

"Shnozberries?" snaps the spoiled, nasty Veruca Salt. "Who ever heard of a shnozberry?"

Confronted with such disrespect, Wonka grabs her cheeks

between his thumb and forefinger and turns her face to him. With her tongue still sticking out and conspicuously orange from the delicious lick of a wallpaper fruit, she is forced to look Mr. Wonka directly in the eye. As he stares her down, he scolds in a deliberately slow, authoritative voice, "We are the music-makers, and we are the dreamers of the dreams."

Clearly, the creator of this wonderful wallpaper—indeed, of the entire amazing factory—is not about to be mocked by a child who, because of her own narrow understanding of the world, has no idea how things work at the Chocolate Factory.[2]

Veruca Salt had been given the opportunity for the adventure of a lifetime. Little did she know she was actually being tested by the great Willy Wonka as a candidate to inherit the entire factory. Unfortunately for Veruca, her own disbelief and arrogance cut her off from the adventure that could have been.

Sometimes we stare our Creator in the face and, out of pure ignorance and disbelieving arrogance, we do something even worse than Veruca did: we disdainfully proclaim that *we* know better how to live our lives than the One who created us does. My purpose in writing this book is to convince you otherwise. I believe the most satisfying life you can have is one where you say *yes* to your Creator's plan for your life.

What if you said yes to a single decision that would change everything and set you on an amazing adventure you never dreamed possible? What if that *yes* were actually the perfect path God had planned for your life?

The reality is, you are one yes away from living a life of true adventure. In the pages ahead, I will describe a path God took me on to learn some simple truths that changed everything.

So, what *have* I learned?

LOVE

I have learned to see God as He *really* is and, as a result, live a life of *love*.

For most of my life I had an inaccurate view of God. I viewed Him as a kindly friend who was desperate for me to squeeze Him into my busy life, instead of recognizing Him as the immense, all-powerful, unfathomable, epic Emperor of the universe—who *loves* me. If I'd had an accurate view of God, I would not have lived the lackadaisical, lackluster, uninspired Christian life I lived for so many years.

If the president of the United States of America showed up at your house, knocked on your door, and invited you to accompany him on a trip around the world, would you say, "Sorry, Mr. President, but my schedule won't allow it. I can't miss my tennis game today, and after that I was going to catch up on my newspaper reading for the week"? That response would be unlikely. No matter what your political persuasion, the position of the president of the United States demands respect and immediate action. You would drop everything.

Compared to God, the president is like a pathetic grasshopper. Yet, why would we be willing to drop everything for the creation, and be unwilling to change anything for the loving Creator and Sustainer of all?

In this book you will see how a right view of our massive yet affectionate God changes everything. When we truly begin to comprehend the depths of His majesty, we will be in awe of His enormous love for us. Gratitude for such amazing, undeserved love will compel us to give of ourselves and our treasure. His inexplicable love toward us will become the motivation for all we do. When we consistently view Him as He really is, the rewards—wealth, fame, glory, and position—of worldly success are bizarrely dim in comparison to being in a deep love relationship with our almighty Creator.

SKIP

Through a series of events that you will read about in these pages, I learned to *skip*.

Every human love relationship involves giving. The same thing is true of our relationship with our Creator; our response to being loved *by* God should be to give love *to* God and others. Sadly, in the past, too often for me, it was not. While I was willing to sacrificially give to my husband and children, when it came to God, I all too often failed to give anything but leftovers. That's where skipping comes in.

Skipping something for the sake of someone less fortunate is the kind of giving that illustrates God's love. If I skip a lunch to feed a hungry child, the child gets fed. That's fabulous. But even more, an attitude and a lifestyle of giving can make life truly thrilling. It may defy human wisdom, but the true gift really does belong to the giver.

I recently saw a sign that said, "You have never really lived until you have done something for someone who can never repay you." The truth is, a life characterized by *skipping* leads to a life of exhilaration and authentic fulfillment.

JUMP

Finally, I have learned that the essence of saying yes to God is *jumping*—using your God-given gifts to affect others. *Jumping* is an action, a choice in your life to do something to serve God and the people around you. Jumping changes your life from one of spiritual consumerism to a life of *doing*.

God has some amazing life adventures set out for each of us. The challenge is, we must say *yes* to Him and take the *jump* into action. I invite you to join me on this journey. As you read the following pages, it is my prayer that you will be open, and I hope you are inspired to seek, find, and *jump* into the adventure God has always had planned for you but you have failed to yet seize.

Are you willing to say *yes* to that?

ONE

The Adventure of Yes

It was my typical I-love-to-have-tons-of-people-over-for-no-reason kind of party. Our friends inviting their friends, they, in turn, inviting theirs, and so on. This party looked and felt just like another fun night. Little did I know that the evening's events would change everything.

After tending to my guests, I was standing in my kitchen, talking with a group of gals. A woman I'd never met before pointed to my refrigerator. On the door hung pictures of the two kids we sponsor in Africa: a little Ugandan girl named Omega, for our daughter, Brooke; and an adorable Ugandan boy named Alonis, for our son, Blake—all to teach our kids how blessed they are, living in America. Boldly, the woman said, "You fell for that?"

"Excuse me?"

"How do you know that those kids on your refrigerator are real?" she continued. "They might be forty years old, and they are just taking your money."

Shocked, I said, "I don't. I guess I'm just having faith that the money's getting there." Inside I was thinking, *What is your name, and can you get out of my house?* Gotta love your inside voice.

1

She proceeded to boast, "Yeah, well, I never fall for those things."

That night, after all the party guests were gone, I was left with a nagging, unsettled feeling. I could not get that woman's words out of my head. What if what she said was true? What if we were being scammed?

When I got into bed, I shook my husband, Brice, awake. He groggily glared at me with a "This better be important" look. I told him about our nameless guest and her comments about forty-year-olds in Africa stealing our kids' money. I then said, "So honey, I want to go to Africa and see where our twenty-five bucks a month is going."

He said, "Cool. Let's spend three thousand dollars so you can see where our twenty-five bucks a month is going."

"Brice, I'm serious. What if it's fake and we've been telling our kids that we've been sponsoring these kids in Uganda and instead we've been paying for some guy's Porsche?"

"Any chance we can talk about this in the morning?" he said with a groggy smile.

Well, the man's been married to me for a while, and he agreed we could get the information and we could check it out. And that's exactly what I did. My first call the next day was to our friends, the very same people who'd hooked us up with these sponsored kids in the first place. They had never met their kids either, but they said they were getting ready to take a trip to Uganda and that Brice and I were welcome to tag along.

Since I had put my career in the entertainment industry on hold to be a stay-at-home mom while the kids were little, it was really a matter of convincing Brice to take time off from his growing law practice. Although he was skeptical at first, it did not take too much to convince him this was a worthy adventure. After a thorough discussion we agreed to go.

That decision to go to Africa was my first *yes*. After a lifetime of being over-pampered and unconcerned, I decided I was going to take a risk, get out of my comfort zone, say yes, and go with my husband to the "wild" continent.

Over the next few months, Brice and I made the preparations. We got all the shots. We shopped for mosquito-proof clothes. We bought hiking boots and special fluffy-wicky socks. (According to the shoe salesman, these exorbitantly expensive socks suck moisture away from your feet. He said they would be "perfect" for Africa—it never dawned on me to ask how he would know.) We stocked up on three kinds of hand sanitizer—for use after every encounter with a local—and various types of deet bug repellant (the spray kind, the wipe kind, and a small bottle of carry-anywhere kind).

We bought new, giant, heavy-duty suitcases, large enough not only to fit in all our brand-new "Africa" clothes but also to accommodate a generous stock of granola bars, peanut butter, and bottled water just in case the indigenous food was out of our culinary comfort zone. And we arranged for my parents to come down from Palm Desert to Moorpark, California, to watch our two young children.

After months of preparation, two nights before our departure date I proclaimed to the family, "We are prepared!"

The very next night, just hours before our early-morning departure, my husband became deathly ill. He's rarely sick, but about 3:00 a.m., he looked at me with reddened, fever-glazed eyes and said, "Honey, I can't go. I have no strength to get out of bed."

"Brice, you've just got to suck it up. We have to make it to Heathrow."

"Honey, there's no way I can go."

"It's a sign," I declared. "We were going to die on the plane and leave our two kids orphaned while we try and find these kids in Uganda who are probably forty."

Brice said, "Shelene, you are so dramatic, and you're not sick."

"What are you saying?" I asked.

"I'm saying *you're* not sick. You need to go."

"Brice," I whined, "you are going to send your only wife *alone* to the other side of the world? Who's gonna carry my luggage?"

He got very quiet. Then he said, "Honey, you don't like to go anywhere but the day spa. The fact you want to go to east Africa is astonishing. God obviously wants to take a vacation with you."

With me? Understand, I spent a lot of my Christian life planning events for my family, friends, women's groups, and marriage retreats so people could build relationships or maybe even find God. But God and I had never gone anywhere together alone. I couldn't help but think to myself, *What are God and I going to talk about for ten days?*

Up until this trip, I was probably the safest person you've ever met. I was happy sending a donation check when I'd hear someone wanted to go to the ends of the earth to help the poor, but as for me, I was going to stay right here in the good ole USA. I'd make comments like, "I want to see my own country before I travel outside of it," or "God would have to rip the roof off the church before I would ever go to a third-world country." On more than a few occasions I made the excellent point, "Somebody has to stay here to make money so others can go." It sure sounded good, and I had convinced myself of the wisdom of these statements.

I don't remember when comfort and safety became my number one priorities, but somehow they had, and I was wholly unaware it was paralyzing me.

As I sat on the edge of our bed, touching my husband's feverish forehead repeatedly with the quickly diminishing hope that the raging fever would break, I knew I had a decision to make. What was I going to do? All my dreams and plans about this trip had always included my husband—my rock and my protector. But now it was painfully obvious he would not be going.

It was at that moment, sitting on the edge of our bed, that I (with the help of my husband's quiet, calm confidence) said *yes* to God and made the decision to *go*!

I knew I had to go to Uganda. I had really felt that was what God had wanted me to do, and yes, I would go.

The next morning when I woke up, I immediately did the forehead check on Brice, and with no miraculous healing for my husband, I loaded up into a black town car and headed off to LAX with my new, heavy-duty suitcases packed full to the brim.

I boarded a plane from LAX to Heathrow, from Heathrow to Entebbe, then took a bus to the fishing village of Gaba in Uganda east Africa. No one but my husband knew the real reason I was coming. All I had were the pictures I had ripped off my refrigerator and the numbers and names on the back of the photos. But I was going to be Diane Sawyer and blow this thing up if it was fake.

When we arrived in Gaba, I was surprised to see a group from the local church there to greet us. They offered us water and strange fruits, which I happily declined in favor of my bottled water and granola bars. I inquired about where to get information about my children, and a young man pointed at a little open-windowed hut that was apparently the sponsorship office. I made a beeline for that office and burst in, in typical Los Angeles aggressive fashion.

"Hi. I'm from America," I announced, "and I came to meet my two kids, AR212 and GR479."

The woman behind the desk got up and said, "Follow me."

Looking back now, I think if anyone had burst into my office like that, I would have pointed to the door and demanded he get out. Make an appointment for later in the week—my schedule is far too busy to see you.

Not this woman. In a gracious manner and without hesitation, she had jumped up and we started walking . . . and walking and walking.

About half a mile into the hike on a red dirt footpath, I realized I'd just violated about seventeen rules of traveling safety that I had skimmed over before the trip. All travel safety guides would tell you *not* to do everything I had just done. I had left my group, telling no one I was leaving. I was following a complete stranger, and I had no idea where the heck I was. In that moment of mental panic, I realized I did not even know this woman's name. I figured since my life was at her mercy, at least I should know that much about her.

"Oh, by the way," I blurted out, "my name is Shelene. What's your name?"

She smiled a big, warm smile, introduced herself, and continued walking. It felt like she had picked up the pace, and I was really wishing I hadn't dropped out of that kick-boxing class that had seemed at the time a little over the top. Eventually, after what seemed to be a two-mile marathon through the jungle, she stopped abruptly and pointed. "This is Omega's house."

Omega, the little girl from my refrigerator. As I looked up, I did not see a "house" at all—it was anything but a house. It was a red, mud-walled hut the size of my walk-in closet, with a tattered sheet for a front door. My new friend said, "Go ahead. Go in."

As I pulled the sheet back to go inside, I was shaking. This was too real. I stepped off the dirt path and onto the dirt floor of this one-room hut. There was no electricity, no lights, no running water. I had passed the "kitchen" outside the hut. It consisted of hot coals from a fire and one pot sitting on a large stone in the midst of the fire.

Suddenly a little girl in a cute, blue school uniform darted at me with her arms wide open, shrieking, *"Muzunga!"* which means white, but at the time I thought she was saying, "Angel!" because this white girl had just dropped from the sky.

"Omega?" I didn't immediately recognize her because she had grown so much since her photo.

"Yes."

"I'm Shelene."

She smiled shyly. "I know."

I got down on my knees and embraced her. As I hugged her there, a Christmas card photo of my family embedded in her mud wall caught my eye. I unexpectedly had this overwhelming rush of emotion. *This is real*, I thought. *It's really real . . . and she's been getting our mail.* As tears streamed down my cheeks, the realization that this little girl was probably alive due to the tiny sacrifice my kids had made every month hit me like a ton of bricks. My children skipping a video game, a meal out, or forgoing the latest fad toy was actually keeping this beautiful little girl alive, fed, and in school.

Still overwhelmed, I said, "Omega, I'll get you anything. What do you want, honey?"

She stood there for a moment, looking at me with her big brown eyes, and then she gasped. A huge smile spread across her face and she said, "A bed."

A bed? Cool . . . Where's Target jungle?

––––––

The next day I went to meet Alonis, the young boy we'd been sponsoring. He, like Omega, had been receiving the one meal per day provided at school but was sleeping on a woven reed mat on the hard-packed, red mud ground. That morning I took Alonis and Omega into Kampala, the bustling capital of Uganda. They had never been out of their village, so to see the city was quite a shock.

We made our way into an open-air flea market. The "shops" were set up like little booths in the dirt. Cardboard, sheets, broken pieces of wood, and corrugated metal siding were haphazardly placed between the stalls. Soon the shopkeepers began calling out to us.

There were women with a few varieties of half-wilted vegetables piled high on tables. There were butchers with not-so-freshly killed meats, fly covered and hanging for inspection and purchase. Handwoven traditional African tunics were thrust at us and draped over us whether we welcomed them or not. Crudely carved figurines and trinkets fashioned from reeds and corn husks were held up in front of our faces. All the vendors were frenziedly beckoning us into their booths, recognizing that with the Americans, a month's wages could be made with one sale if we could be enticed by their goods.

Eventually we made our way to a vendor who had a stack of thin mattresses piled up outside of his booth. Omega ran excitedly over, put her hand down on the not-so-soft foam, and looked back at me with a twinkle of enthusiasm in her eye. I gave her a reassuring nod and asked the man how much for a mattress. To my amazement, he stated that they were three dollars each.

He also pulled out bedsheets and mosquito nets designed to drape over the beds to keep out mosquitoes, which routinely carried malaria. He then pointed out a pair of shoes that would fit Omega and gave us the total price for the bed, sheets, nets, and shoes: twenty bucks.

I said, "Well, sir, at that price I would like to buy *all* the beds in your store."

I thought the store owner was going to have a heart attack. His eyes filled with tears, and he was exuding pure delight.

"God bless you! Oh, God bless you! My wife is pregnant, and you must be an angel, for I know God sent you to my store."

His immediate faith and credit to God for bringing us to his little stall gave me the chills. It was at this instant, as he was thanking me for cleaning out his shop, that I could almost feel God whisper in my ear, *"Shelene, are you having fun yet?"*

Fun? Are you kidding? This was one of the top ten moments of my life!

I was experiencing firsthand the verse in the Bible that says, "It is better to give than receive" (Acts 20:35, paraphrased). So far, I had only applied that verse at Christmastime, when my kids had sat at the foot of the Christmas tree with an immense pile of gifts. But now, the reality of that truth hit me in a way I had never felt before.

So I got another bright idea: I decided to go back to Omega's village and do an HGTV design on a real dime.

And that's exactly what I did: a little "extreme village make-over," and it cost almost nothing. I started passing out mattresses like a deck of cards and rolling out linoleum on the mud floors and putting up mosquito nets in the villagers' sleeping areas.

As we passed out these gifts to the villagers, I could not help thinking about my over-pampered friends back home where beds were not just three-inch hunks of cheap foam but works of technological innovation. Ours has computer-controlled air-pressure chambers, where the ambient air pressure is constantly monitored to maintain the exact pound per square inch over the surface area of our bodies, and of course, separate chambers and controls for me and my spouse in case his sense of perfect comfort is a few pounds less stiff than my idea of perfect comfort. If my friends and family could just see the joy in this little girl due to a three-dollar piece of foam, I just knew they would do something.

I was struck with the thought that if everyone back home could truly understand this was a *real* life-and-death struggle for *real* people, they would be willing to help. If they could realize that skipping their own indulgences and giving those resources would keep a child alive, they'd skip them. For my friends, twenty-five dollars was something to spend on frivolities. For these African children, that money is the difference between starving to death and being fed, schooled, and having clothes to wear.

In looking back at how I said yes to God that first time and went to Africa, I would have to say that some of the most amazing things God wants to do in our lives as Christians involve giving Him permission to take us on uncomfortable journeys. My journey was a literal journey to Africa—yours might be different. My desire is for you to join me on a *yes* adventure that will make you uncomfortable.

The fact is, every significant event that happened in the Bible happened because somebody said *yes* to God. Noah said yes to God and built an ark, despite the mocking of every person he knew—and was saved. Moses said yes to God when, at great personal risk, he demanded freedom for his people—and they were freed. David said yes when he fought Goliath—and later he became king of Israel. Esther saved her people from annihilation . . . Peter stepped over the side of a small fishing boat and walked on water . . . and Jesus paid the price for your failings and mine *forever.* It all happened when they each said *yes* to God.

My question to you is this: Are you saying *yes* to what God has for you in your life? As I look back, I have realized that saying yes to God started a progression of favor from Him that has led to an incredible series of adventures. I said yes to the desire God put on my heart to go see if my sponsored kids were real; my husband said yes to us going to Uganda; I said yes to getting out of my comfort zone and going without him; and each and every *yes* was an opportunity for a great adventure in Christ.

What incredible opportunity awaits you? Are you willing to say *yes*?

Lord, give me the wisdom to recognize the comforts that constrain my desire to follow You. Help me seek above all else the things You would have me do in my life. Help me identify the yes opportunities You are putting in my path. Amen.

TWO

Can You Hear Me Now?

When I got back home to Los Angeles, my phone rang off the hook with calls from my girlfriends. "Were those kids real?" "Did you get sick?" "Did you see _____ [take your pick: lions, elephants, monkeys, zebras, wildebeests, Pumbaa]?" "When can I see your pictures?"

To avoid retelling the story several hundred times, I decided to have an Africa party. I know most girls have Tupperware, Longaberger, or Pampered Chef parties, but not me. I had an Africa party and invited sixty of my girlfriends over for a luncheon. I shared with them 10 of the 168 Bible passages I had recently discovered about the poor. I shared with them the photos and stories. But most of all, I shared my heart.

With passion in my voice, I explained to this group of ladies that while I was on the plane to Uganda, I met the founder of Children's Hunger Fund, Dave Phillips. It's crazy, because the man attended my church and only lives eleven miles from my house, but I had never met him.

God's ways are rarely our ways, a point clearly illustrated by the fact that God had to rip me out of my Southern California shopping-mall comfort zone and drop me on the other side of the world to introduce me to Dave. Even though Dave and I were practically neighbors, God had big plans that had nothing to do with our little Southern California community. Dave was not part of my group, but just by happenstance—or divine intervention—he had booked a ticket on the same plane. He also "happened" to be booked in the seat right next to mine. Sitting next to Dave for the twenty-four-hour trip let God's plan spark and then simmer.

Children's Hunger Fund (CHF) is an amazing ministry that brings food to children in need around the world. It was such an eye-opener to meet Dave and see that he and his team were over in Uganda doing exactly what they claimed to do. CHF was supporting a local church in Gaba led by Pastor Peter Kasiriva.

Dave invited me to join Pastor Peter to help pass out food packs. A food pack is a box, about the size of an extra-tall shoe box, filled with high-quality food: beans, pasta, rice, and so forth. We needed to get the food across Lake Victoria to a place called Bethany Village, which was little more than an open plot of land on a peninsula jutting out from the mainland into the lake.

I said, "Let's do it. I'm in." Little did I know what I was "in" for. I arranged to meet up with Dave and his team a few days later.

When the time came, we walked through the busy fish market of Gaba, treated once again to all the delightful sights and smells of fish guts from freshly disemboweled and day-old fish, and ended our short walk at the welcoming shores of beautiful Lake Victoria. After being awed by the largest tropical lake in the world (with a surface area of 26,600 square miles and the origin of the mighty Nile river) and equally relieved to get away from the fish guts, I was directed by our guide to a group of people standing by what from far off appeared to be a cluster of logs floating together on the shoreline. As I walked closer to the logs, I realized that what I'd thought were logs were actually wooden boats, and that those boats were going to be my mode of transportation to Bethany Village. We piled into the boats and set off on the lake.

As the boats whisked through the waves following the shoreline, I couldn't help but think I was on the real jungle ride cruise at Disneyland. But when I mentioned how wonderful it would be to see a "cute little hippo," my host glared at me with a scowl and said in a heavily accented voice, "My fair lady, *hope* we see no hippos." He proceeded to inform me that hippos kill more people than lions kill in the jungle. Yikes.

As our journey began to slow and we moved toward the shoreline of Bethany Village, two muscle-bound locals, who looked like fitness models, walked out into the water to receive our boat. The shoreline was different from where we had boarded. Here there was beautiful grass at the water's edge but no easy place to debark. Our guide warned us not to touch the water because of the "nasty parasites and leeches."

As the boats landed shoreside, the male "fitness models" began lifting us out and carrying us to land. When I realized that Mr. Universe was about to lift me from the boat, I was feeling pretty bad about the extra thirty pounds I was carrying. I thought, *Geesh! Had I known about this, I would have joined that boot camp when my girlfriends invited me.* I quickly turned to Pastor Peter's wife, Mamma Irene.

"I thought you said your vision was to turn this village into what I like to call a 'little house on the prairie' village, with a school, orphan houses with land to grow crops, and a youth camp for surrounding villages to come and hear about God."

She smiled. "Oh yes, Mamma Shelene. That's exactly what we're going to do."

"Well then, you're going to need a dock. I know these guys are strong and all, but I don't think people are going to want to be lifted out of the boat every time they come over to visit the children."

"That's very true," Pastor Peter sheepishly replied.

"So, how much is a dock?"

He responded, "Oh, it's very expensive."

I thought, *Look, I just bought beds for three bucks, so it can't be too much. This just might be doable.* Instead I said, "Okay, but how much is 'very expensive'?"

"Four hundred US dollars?"

"Done!" I proclaimed. I pulled out my wallet and counted out four crisp one-hundred-dollar bills. I was still in the process of learning that God's solution to difficult circumstances does not necessarily involve our financial resources.

As shock covered Pastor Peter's smiling face, I said, "If I ever come back here, Pastor, I want to be able to exit the boat by myself onto that new dock."

With laughter in his voice, he said, "Okay. Thank you, Mamma Shelene."

"No . . . thank *you*, Pastor." I felt as if I were walking on air.

We all grabbed the food packs and started hiking into the bush.

As we arrived at what our interpreter called "Fishers Village," I began to head in to meet the children. Our guide grabbed my arm and said, "Wait. We need to be invited in by the chief first."

"The *chief*? There is really a chief?" I asked.

16

"Oh yes. It would be a slight not to ask permission to enter his village," he said.

I stood there in disbelief. *What the heck am I doing here?* I thought to myself. *This is crazy.* Standing there, just waiting, fear crept in. I began whispering to God, "Lord, am I ever going to see my husband and kids again? Why am I here?"

It seemed like an eternity, but in a matter of minutes, we got permission to enter the village. Up until this time, I had met Omega and Alonis and seen their mud huts. I had been to the largest Ugandan city, Kampala. I had visited some really sick kids with malaria in Gaba village. But this village made those other villages and cities look like an advanced, modern metropolis. I walked in carrying my food packs and quickly spotted a four-year-old little boy with a recent burn on his forearm so severe that his skin was peeling off.

I asked the interpreter, "What happened?"

He said the little boy had fallen into the fire a few nights earlier, and the villagers had tried to treat the wound by putting salt on it. *Ouch!*

"This boy needs medical attention," I announced.

"Yes, yes, he does," the interpreter said, "but there is no one who can help."

I felt so helpless. I could do nothing but hug this beautiful little boy and pray over him, leaving him in God's hands to keep infection away.

If I can't help this boy, what am I doing here? I asked myself.

As I was trying to hold back the tears, another little boy, about seven, slowly walked up to me with a huge smile on his face. His stomach was sticking out like a nine-month-pregnant woman about to give birth.

I looked at the interpreter and asked, "What's wrong with his stomach?"

"He is starving to death."

"This can't happen. I'm from America, and I have an American Express card. What can we do? I will pay for treatment—whatever is needed."

"Mamma Shelene, if we were in the United States, yes, there would be options, but there are no options out here in the jungle."

"What do you mean? How is that possible?" I asked.

He then explained that the little boy was so hungry that his inside organs were eating themselves, just like a baby in its mother's womb—if the mom isn't providing the nutrients the baby needs, it will take them from the mom. This boy's tummy was bloated from the lack of food and was filled with pus from infection.

"How long does he have?"

"How long will you be here?"

"Ten days," I replied.

He pursed his lips and nodded. "That's about all the time he has left."

No! I screamed inside. The anguish I felt at that moment for this boy was overpowering. I felt such a sense of helplessness. It was too late. Nothing could be done to save him. If I had only arrived a week earlier, our food packs might have saved him. He didn't have AIDS or cancer; he was dying of hunger. Up until that moment in my life, I had only known of people dying as a consequence of *over*eating. And now here I was, face-to-face with impending death because of starvation.

As the day went on, a lingering question began to gnaw at my thoughts: *What are you doing here?*

Am I just supposed to see this misery and go home and continue to live my life pretending it's not real, my inner voice continued, *going from my posh, air-conditioned house to my posh, air-conditioned luxury car to the posh, air-conditioned mall? Am I to just forget that this boy is almost dead and will be dead before I leave for home? Am I to forget that these kids have no hope?*

What are you doing here?

We continued passing out food packs, but within an hour we were out of food.

I was dumbfounded—there was still a massive need. These villagers and children still *needed* food, but we were entirely out.

In a week or two these kids, who had just accepted our food and who were playing in front of me now, could be just like the youngster who was going to die in the next few days. Another kid who at this moment is laughing and running right before my eyes might die because we simply could not carry enough food from Gaba. I interrupted my solitary self-pity session and blurted out loud, "That is unacceptable!"

"Why are you here?" breathed the quiet voice.

It was that quiet, small voice, which had at first sounded like mine, that I now realized was very unlike my voice. It's amazing how when you're uncomfortable and in uncomfortable surroundings, you need God in a whole new way, and how His quiet voice that softly examines you can finally be heard. That powerful need for your Creator becomes glaringly apparent when you are ill at ease and helpless. It is in those times of helplessness that the need for the Father, who specifically crafted you for the tasks He has set out for you, those tasks for which you have been specifically gifted and that you will love to do for Him, becomes clear. It is in those moments of destitution that His voice finally becomes clear.

I had been observing for days various pastors, caregivers, and teachers carrying food by hand into outlying villages. I'd witnessed children waking up early in the morning and walking for miles just to fetch some not-so-safe drinking water in containers nearly as tall as they were. One local pastor had told me of walking fifteen miles loaded up with all the food packs he could carry.

At that moment the answer came to me, the answer to the question that had been hounding my thoughts all day. It seemed too simple to be real. *Bikes*, I thought. *We need bikes with carrying racks, and we need to mobilize everyone we know to supply them.*

You see, to walk fifteen miles on a jungle path takes nearly half a day, but to ride fifteen miles on a bicycle takes a little more than an hour and a half. Someone walking can carry two food packs at most, but a bike equipped with a carrying rack can transport six. Food packs can be loaded onto several bikes' carrying racks and ride ten times the food directly to the children. If the little boy with the death sentence had been visited by a caretaker riding a bike rather than walking, there might have been enough food to keep him alive until we arrived.

Then the small voice said, *"Are you going to do it?"* And without hesitation I said out loud, *"Yes,* Lord, *yes* to bikes!"

When I got back to our hotel, I began to brainstorm about the bikes and I started thinking about all the bicycles sitting in my friends' garages, collecting dust. What if people back home sold their unused bikes and donated the money so we could buy jungle bikes for these locals? I shared my "jungle ride" idea with Dave Phillips and he loved it. That was the inception of the Jungle Ride program, where donors could buy a bike to help pastors, teachers, and caregivers deliver food and medicine to those in need.

Fast-forward one month. There I was, standing in my living room and sharing this story with a good five dozen of my girlfriends from an assortment of Southern California clubs and groups—tennis club members, a political women's group, country club acquaintances, and Hollywood socialites. All these ladies were seated in rapt attention. "In closing, I want to challenge you to buy a bike for eighty-five dollars. Just like we drive a car, all they need is a bike. We can save the lives of these children—we really can."

You can only imagine the dumbfounded looks on my girlfriends' faces as they sat on the very comfortable chairs in my living room, dining on a luxurious spread of food, including Chinese chicken salad, catered by the Cheesecake Factory. As I looked out over that group, there was shock and awe on their faces. Some jaws were slightly dropped; some eyes were swollen and red; some simply showed signs of disbelief that this girl they once knew, who had formerly only cared about herself and the next movie deal or upcoming breakout actor or actress, was actually talking to them about saving the lives of kids in Africa. Was this the same woman who did not like hotels without room service?

"What can we do, Shelene?" asked one. "How can we help?" another ventured. After hearing my stories and seeing the photographs, their loving, compassionate hearts were full, and then I hit them with the *big* one.

"Well, girls," I announced, "I'm going back to Uganda to give out bikes and food. Who's in? Leave your Louis Vuitton bags at home, ladies. Let's change the world together, one village at a time."

In the years that followed that first trip to Africa, I have often reflected on why I recognized God's whispering voice to me as I sat watching a doomed child in Fishers Village. I have come to the conclusion that to hear God, you have to learn to listen. God often speaks with a quiet voice but always speaks in truth. Many do not have ears to hear Him.

I think it is important to note here that I have never heard an audible voice, just a strong sense that a particular thought is from the Lord. I think it is imperative when you think you have heard from God and that He put a thought in your mind, that you *do not assume* that thought is actually from God without serious examination.

The first thing I do when I sense God is leading me in a direction is to compare my thoughts with the Scriptures. As humans, we are fallible and easily capable of self-delusion. That is why we have to measure every thought we think might be from God against the only infallible measure we have: the Bible. If you think God has put a thought in your mind and that thought is inconsistent with or explicitly contradicts what the Bible says, you can be assured that you are acting on your own desires, not God's.

GOD'S WHISPER

One of my favorite Bible characters is a man named Elijah. Elijah had a deep love of God. But the Bible describes his nemesis, King Ahab, as a wicked king, who did more evil in the eyes of the Lord than all the wicked kings before him. His malicious wife, Queen Jezebel, had systematically murdered hundreds of men of God in Israel, and Elijah felt he was the only man of God left. Ahab and Jezebel were on a mission to find and kill Elijah. King Ahab sent out soldiers to every town and village in a nationwide manhunt, and even sent them to hunt for Elijah in the neighboring countries.

In the midst of this massive manhunt, Elijah needed God's intervention more than ever. So what did he do?

Did he rally his friends in search of help?

Did he try to unite the armies of Ahab's enemies?

Did he hide out in the houses of his supporters?

No, he left his only friend and traveling companion, his servant, in town and ventured alone into the wilderness for the sole purpose of seeking God.

When God finally spoke to Elijah, it was through a quiet whisper in the midst of a series of riotous distractions.

> Then a great and powerful wind tore the mountains apart and shattered the rocks before the LORD, but the LORD was not in the wind. After the wind was an earthquake, but the LORD was not in the earthquake. After the earthquake came a fire, but the LORD was not in the fire. *And after the fire came a gentle whisper.* When Elijah heard it, he pulled his cloak over his face and went out and stood at the mouth of the cave [where he'd been hiding]. Then a voice said to him, "What are you doing here, Elijah?" (1 Kings 19:11–13, emphasis added)

Can you imagine a wind powerful enough to tear apart a mountain and strong enough to shatter rocks? Can you imagine what kind of sound a wind like that would make? Do you think a rock-smashing hurricane like that would compete for your attention over someone whispering gently to you? What about an earthquake?

Being a Southern California native, I have been in my fair share of earthquakes, and, believe me, when the very ground beneath you begins to move like a wave in the ocean, the gripping fear that can overtake you could easily distract you away from a gentle whisper.

Often we cannot hear God's gentle whisper because we allow the noise of our surroundings to choke out any possibility of recognizing His voice.

There are so many voices calling out to us, distracting us. These voices are not necessarily advocating bad things, but they can become very loud and demanding. They could be the screaming of our society's materialism—bigger, better, more luxurious homes, cars, and assorted stuff. Workaholism—fifty-five, sixty, seventy hours of work in a week. It could be allowing things and activities to crowd out any "still" in your life.

Soccer, tennis, football, returning e-mails, video games, television, and Facebook—these are not inherently bad things but can become voices of constant, unending noise dominating our listening and thwarting any possibility that we will hear God's gentle whisper. The reality is that in our modern society we have virtual choirs of voices pulling us, distracting us from His gentle whisper that beckons.

HEARING GOD'S CALL

In Revelation 3:20, Jesus says, "Here I am! I stand at the door and knock. *If anyone hears my voice* and opens the door, I will come in and eat with that person and they with me" (emphasis added).

It is significant that Jesus prefaces that promise with "*if* anyone hears my voice . . ." This verse makes it clear that people are missing His voice all the time. Certainly this verse is Jesus' call out of spiritual death into eternal life with Him. But I don't think Jesus' calling is a onetime, exclusive call to a relationship with God.

Once you are in a love relationship with your Creator, His voice does not stop calling simply because you are in right relationship with Him. God's call to the believer is for fellowship with Him, and His call is as diverse as we are. His call to you may also be the specific assignment He wants to give you and for which He is preparing you.

The real question is, are you hearing His call? Are you listening? Have you *learned* to listen so you can hear Him in the midst of rock-smashing winds, earthquakes, fires, final exams, college applications, Instagrams, television, tweets, Facebook, text messages, phone calls, mortgage payments, retirement funding, and credit card bills? Or do you have to get uncomfortable and distraction-free to learn to listen to the voice of God? I did. Elijah did.

In Psalm 46:10, God is speaking, and He says, "Be still, and know that I am God." When was the last time *you* were still? When was the last time you stilled the voices around you so you could know that He is God and have even a hope of recognizing His voice?

When I learned to listen, I realized that God's voice of truth is the only voice worth listening to. I dare you to get distraction-free and listen for God's voice. His gentle whisper is often too quiet to be heard in a culture that never stops and is never still. God is not like the guy in the Verizon commercials, asking, "Can you hear me now? . . . Can you hear me now? . . . Can you hear me now?" with every single step. No, God's quiet voice of truth softly beckons, and He really does want us to hear His call.

DON'T BE A "YES MAN" TO EVERYTHING

In the movie *Yes Man*, Jim Carrey plays a depressed bank loan executive who says no to everything from bank loans to any opportunity for spontaneous fun ever presented to him. He is challenged by a charismatic, and somewhat creepy, motivational guru to say *yes* to literally everything for an entire year. "Every time an opportunity presents itself," the man basically tells him, "you will say . . . *yes*."

This sets up some very funny situations, in which Carrey's character, Carl, cannot say no—like the toothless Persian woman from an online dating service, who makes a marriage proposal he is obligated to accept. The dare to snort hot sauce up his nose was particularly entertaining. In time, Carl finds himself involuntarily saying yes to learning Korean, taking guitar lessons, throwing a baby shower, and bungee jumping off a bridge.

Saying yes to everything obviously becomes problematic and is not what I am talking about.

What I am talking about is listening to God's call and recognizing the things He wants you to say *yes* to, then actually doing those things. We need to learn to listen to His whisper and respond with a yes to the voice of truth, because when God speaks, He calls us to do the most amazing things that will fulfill our hearts like nothing else.

But we can't say *yes* to God without being able to hear His call, and we can't hear His call if we are not listening.

Lord, allow me to know You well enough so that I can recognize Your whisper. Give me the strength of mind to hide Your Word in my heart so I can match Your Word against the voices of my culture. Give me the ability to be still and reflect on who You are and what You have done and what You want to do through me. Amen.

THREE

Massive God, Epic Love

A TRIP TO HEAVEN

What would happen if you could actually visit God for five minutes? Imagine what it would be like if you had a chance to go to heaven and experience the presence of God. The exhilaration of launching through space and time faster than the speed of light toward the immense heavenly dwelling of God would be awesome.

Suddenly you are hurled into the presence of almighty God, and you collapse to the golden-crystalline floor of God's throne room. The light emitting from the throne is brighter than any light you have ever seen, a thousand times brighter than the sun.

Flashes of intense lightning are bolting from the throne. Claps of thunder rumble, shaking the floor beneath you like an earthquake. You see a gigantic throne made of stunning crystal-clear jewels. A foaming white river is gushing from the throne, making Niagara Falls look like a mere trickle.

The train of God's robe flows down and around from the

base of His throne and fills the entire room with giant fields of fabric. You can't speak. You can't stand. Every molecule of air has been sucked from your lungs, and you can't breathe.

You notice the entire scene is encircled by angels—ten thousand times ten thousand of them. One hundred *million* angels. They are visibly powerful beings, and they are passionately singing in spectacular harmony the most beautiful song you have ever heard.

Then you see and hear four wonderfully strange living creatures, special angels who are devoted to calling out majestic acclaim to the one true God. They are stunningly beautiful, each with six wings, one with the head of a lion, one of an ox, one of an eagle, and one of a man. They are suspended above God's throne, flying with two wings and shielding their faces and feet from the light with the other four wings.

"Holy, holy, holy is the Lord God Almighty, who was, and is, and is to come," the creatures cry. Their deep, powerful shouts vibrate everything. Their voices penetrate and pulsate you to the core.

Unexpectedly you hear your name. It's Him. He is speaking your name. His voice is so powerful, so gentle, yet so commanding and loving. You are in awe.

In the presence of this massive God, you suddenly realize how foolish you have been to give Him so little of your attention, how foolish everyone has been to virtually ignore Him. Even those who claim to love God are foolish, so distracted they just don't understand, they just do not know. They never could have imagined this massive God (see Isaiah 6 and Revelation 4, 21, and 22).

OUR RESPONSE TO A MASSIVE GOD: LOVE

Wouldn't a trip to heaven like that be an amazing experience? Can you imagine how your life would be changed if it actually happened to you? Would you agree that spending five minutes with God as I just described would change everything in your life?

My next question is, why? *Why* would it change everything?

Spending five minutes in the presence of the Most High God would alter our lives forever because our view of who God is would unavoidably change from small to epic. In those few moments in heaven, we would embrace the reality that being loved by and loving this unfathomable God is the highest achievement we can possibly obtain in life. Most of us don't live our lives with that reality driving our decisions.

J. I. Packer identifies our problem:

"Your thoughts of God are too human," said Luther to Erasmus. This is where most of us go astray, our thoughts of God are not great enough; we fail to reckon with the reality of his limitless wisdom and power. Because we ourselves are limited and weak, we imagine that at some points God is too, and find it hard to believe that he is not. We think of God as too much like what we are.[1]

EPIC LOVE

It is impossible to fathom the significance of God's love when we have shrunk almighty God down to no more than a glorified Superman. The fact that such a majestic God does not treat us like ants to be crushed is wonderful and phenomenal all at the same time.

He has every right to not bother with us, His creation. He is so set apart from us we cannot begin to comprehend Him any more than an ant can comprehend us. The most fascinating thing about this awesome, all-powerful God is that He takes an immense interest in us, in you and me, right now.

The most unappreciated and ignored declaration of God's love for us is a passage in the Scriptures that we have all heard but often brush over. If you read these verses with fresh eyes, as though you have never heard them, while pondering the scene in the heavenly throne room, I believe you will have a new appreciation for the incomprehensible love God has for us. I know I did.

> For God so loved the world that he gave his one and only Son, that whoever believes in him shall not perish but have eternal life. For God did not send his Son into the world to condemn the world, but to save the world through him. (John 3:16–17)

This mighty God who sits on His throne in spectacular glory sent His only Son to ransom you and me, in spite of ourselves. That is ridiculous love. That is *epic love*.

OUR RESPONSE TO EPIC LOVE: LOVE PEOPLE

> "Teacher, which is the greatest commandment in the Law?"
>
> Jesus replied: "'Love the Lord your God with all your heart and with all your soul and with all your mind.' This is the first and greatest commandment. And the second is like it: 'Love your neighbor as yourself.'" (Matthew 22:36–39)

In light of God's epic love for me, when it comes down to the core meaning of my life, the only factor I live by is the trustworthy words of God's greatest directives: *Love God and love people.*

LOVE PEOPLE

Kendal was just four years old when she collapsed while playing house with her doll in her backyard. Her parents rushed her to the doctor, who referred her immediately to the hospital for a thorough evaluation and testing. After dozens of tests and scans, the doctors advised that Kendal had a rare degenerative kidney disease. Essentially her kidneys were not cleaning her blood, and she was expected to need a kidney transplant within two years or her condition would take her life. She was put on a donor list for a kidney with matching criteria. In the meantime, as a temporary measure, she underwent dialysis treatments to clean her blood each week.

As the months ticked on into a year, it was clear the donor list was a quickly diminishing option. Because of some rare antigens in Kendal's blood, the family was advised by their doctors that a donor list match would be unlikely in time to save Kendal. After testing revealed Kendal's parents were not a match, in desperation the doctor suggested testing Kendal's eight-year-old brother, Kyle, on the slight chance he might be a suitable donor. Kyle's test results came back with all six antigens as an exact match. After a long conversation explaining the procedure, little Kyle was adamant he wanted to give his sister a kidney—he did not want her to die.

The day of the operation came and both children were admitted into the hospital on the same floor. Kyle's procedure to harvest his kidney was to go first and then doctors would implant the donated kidney into his little sister.

Tension was high as the operations began. Several hours later, the doctors came out and announced that things looked to be a great success. Kyle's donated kidney had started working almost immediately during the surgery.

When Kyle was brought back from the recovery room to his hospital room, he wanted to see his mom. As he was resting peacefully, she entered the room. She began rubbing his hair and singing his favorite song. As his eyes fluttered open, a smile came across his face upon seeing his mom.

"Mommy," he asked, "did the doctor save Kendal?"

"Yes, Kyle, thanks to you, Kendal is going to be just fine."

"Oh good, I'm so glad," he said with a sigh. He took a deep breath, looked at his mom, and his lower lip began to protrude as his eyes teared up.

"What's wrong, Kyle? Are you in pain?"

"No, I feel okay."

"Then what's the matter, sweetie?"

"Mommy, I . . . I was just wondering when I am supposed to die?"

"What? Oh, honey, you're not going to die."

"I'm not?" He smiled with relief on his face. "I thought I had to give my kidney to Kendal so she could live."

With a big hug his mom explained that he had two kidneys and he only needed one. He was going to be just fine.

True love is willing to give. Even a child who loves a sibling responds to true love with a giving heart.

I think there are three words in the Bible that define what it means to love people: *that He gave.* These words come from that same verse that holds so much truth, John 3:16: "For God so loved the world *that he gave . . .*"

The result of God's love for us was *that He gave.*

The fact is, God has wired each of us with a completely natural response to love: the act of giving. Whether it is the romantic love of a new boyfriend or girlfriend, the love of a parent for a child, or the love of a brother wanting to save his sister, the God-wired response to love is giving. When every love relationship is examined, you will find giving as a consequence.

The bottom line is: love gives.

So what does it mean to love people? In one sense it means we need to live a life that exemplifies giving to others. Too many people profess to love God, but the only thing they give is lip service. Love is not lip service—it is the motivation to give of yourself. When it really comes down to it, true love always involves giving to others.

If we want to find the adventure God has planned for our lives, we need to imitate God's epic love for us. "For God so loved the world that he *gave . . .*" So our imitation of Him should look something like this:

> For Shelene so loved Omega *that she gave* the money she would have spent every day on Starbucks tea to pay for her education.
>
> For Matt so loved the children of Gaba *that he gave* freely of his time to see that they would have one meal a day.
>
> For Melissa so loved her children *that she gave* the gift of patience and refused to react in anger.
>
> For Michelle so loved her husband, Mark, *that she gave* him her devoted love and attention.

For Deb so loved her friend *that she gave* every Friday morning to study the Bible with her and to help her come to know her Creator.

For Candace so loved her community *that she gave* of her time to serve as a guest chef at a homeless shelter.

I want to challenge you to write out five "that she/he gave" statements of your own.

1. For_____so loved_____that she/he gave _____.
2. For_____so loved_____that she/he gave _____.
3. For_____so loved_____that she/he gave _____.
4. For_____so loved_____that she/he gave _____.
5. For_____so loved_____that she/he gave _____.

The amazing thing is that God's giving nature has not changed. He is still in the giving business. As a reward for those who choose to follow Him, He promises to give even more:

"My Father's house has many rooms; if that were not so, would I have told you that I am going there to prepare a place for you? And if I go and prepare a place for you, I will come back and take you to be with me that you also may be where I am. You know the way to the place where I am going." (John 14:2–4)

This mind-blowing, massive God, whose immeasurable love has rescued us from the consequences of our own rebellion, does not stop giving. In fact, He has gone to prepare another astonishing gift, a place just for you and me. Our response to such a marvelous, giving God is to love Him and give of ourselves to others. I challenge you to put your love of God into action right now.

Lord, help me never lose sight of how powerful and majestic You are. Help me love You with all my heart, from the depths of my soul, and with my entire mind. Help me love the people You bring across my path by giving of my time, my resources, and my heart to point them to You. Amen.

FOUR

You've Got to Jump

After he had dismissed them, he went up on a mountainside by himself to pray. Later that night, he was there alone, and the boat was already a considerable distance from land, buffeted by the waves because the wind was against it. Shortly before dawn Jesus went out to them, walking on the lake. When the disciples saw him walking on the lake, they were terrified. "It's a ghost," they said, and cried out in fear. But Jesus immediately said to them: "Take courage! It is I. Don't be afraid."

"Lord, if it's you," Peter replied, "tell me to come to you on the water."

"Come," he said. Then Peter got down out of the boat, walked on the water and came toward Jesus. But when he saw the wind, he was afraid and, beginning to sink, cried out, "Lord, save me!" Immediately Jesus reached out his hand and caught him. "You of little faith," he said, "why did you doubt?" And when they climbed into the boat, the wind died down. Then those who were in the boat worshiped him, saying, "Truly you are the Son of God." (Matthew 14:23–33)

Peter jumped. That is what I love about this passage, the fact that Peter actually jumped out of the boat. And by jumping, he had the amazing opportunity to walk on water!

There were eleven other disciples who, in the black of night in the midst of a terrifying storm, just like Peter, saw Jesus walking on the water toward them. They, like Peter, all heard Jesus' reassurance: "Take courage! It is I. Don't be afraid."

Eleven didn't jump, but Peter took that leap right out of the comfort and safety of the boat to go be with his Lord. It's not that the other disciples weren't followers of Jesus. Indeed, they were passionate followers, and most would soon lose their lives as a consequence of their true devotion to Jesus. But Peter was willing to do something that no one else was—*jump.*

You have already heard and will hear a lot more in this book about what I believe is the biggest life-obstructing condition of our current generation: comfort and safety. For those of us who have lived our lives way too long in a self-centered "me world," this Bible passage is very instructive. Just like the eleven disciples who did not jump, we each have our own personal "boats" of comfort and safety that keep us from jumping into the exciting waters God has prepared for us. The question is, what is holding you back from being like Peter and making the jump?

John Ortberg has written in his superb book *If You Want to Walk on Water, You've Got to Get Out of the Boat*:

> *What's your boat?*
>
> Your boat is whatever represents safety and security to you apart from God himself. Your boat is whatever you are

tempted to put your trust in, especially when life gets a little stormy. Your boat is whatever keeps you so comfortable that you don't want to give it up even if it's keeping you from joining Jesus on the waves. Your boat is whatever pulls you away from the high adventure of extreme discipleship.[1]

What is holding you back from really jumping in with your Creator?

Your job?

Your spouse?

A relationship?

An addiction?

Success?

The desire to have others perceive you as successful?

A house?

A car?

That college you really want to attend?

For me it was success in business and the admiration of others that came with it. I craved the accolades that accompanied being a successful businesswoman. For many years I fought God on the direction He wanted to take my life because I liked the praise that tickled my ears, and I loved the comfort of luxury.

Recently I had a meeting with a college admittance counselor at my son's high school. This is an amazingly sharp young woman who had received a master's degree from Harvard University. She explained how after graduating from Harvard she got her dream job and went to work in New York City on

Wall Street. After a few years she transferred within her company to the West Coast and had an office with a gorgeous view of the Pacific Ocean.

"My job was to make a lot of rich people a lot richer," she said. In the eyes of most people, she had really arrived. But over time she realized that making rich people richer was not really what God had in mind for her to do with her gifts.

So, she jumped. She took a huge pay cut and went to work helping high school students find the right path for college and pointing them in the direction of a career. Sure, she could use her God-given gifts to make money for people—or she could use those gifts to pour into young people and make a difference in the lives of our future leaders.

After she told us her story, she proceeded to tell us that after that year she was going to be handing us off to a new college admittance counselor.

"Why?" I asked. "We really like you."

"Well, actually, I am moving to South Korea. I accepted a position there with a school to help Korean students find their way."

"Oh, South Korea, that country under daily threat of nuclear annihilation from that wacky North Korean dictator Kim Jong-un?"

This is a girl who is willing to jump.

WHAT IS JUMPING?

So what is jumping? Jumping looks different for every person and in every circumstance, so how can you define what it means to *jump*?

I'm not sure you can fully define what it means to jump, but this is the best I can do: Jumping is an act of your will to use your God-given gifts to affect others. It is an action, a choice followed by movement, a decision resulting in moving feet.

Jumping involves moving from a state of inertia. The dictionary defines *inertia* as resistance to change. Newton's first law of uniform motion states an object *continues* to do whatever it happens to be doing unless a force is exerted upon it. If you are not using your God-given gifts to help others, you've got to expend some energy to get moving. You have got to jump.

When it comes to living the adventure of yes in your relationship with God, the essence of saying yes to God is jumping.

THE COST OF JUMPING

There is a cost to jumping. For Peter, if he could not walk with Jesus on the water, his jump was probably a death sentence. People of Jesus' day did not commonly know how to swim. They would stay out of the water to avoid the threat of drowning. Fishing was a dangerous profession because falling overboard and drowning while pulling in nets filled with fish was common, and it took thousands of lives.

When Peter jumped out of the boat, it was totally unfamiliar territory and the stakes could not have been higher. There was no backup plan to do the breaststroke if the walking thing didn't work out. His was a life-or-death leap of faith. If Jesus was not who Peter believed Him to be, the Son of the living God, Peter would not be returning to the boat.

There is a cost to jumping, but the risks never outweigh the reward, and the cost of not jumping ultimately will be even greater. Some will count the cost of jumping to be too high, but I can assure you that Peter never regretted that experience of walking on water with Jesus.

THREE TYPES OF WANNABE JUMPERS

A lot of Christians are wannabe jumpers. Pretenders. Fakers. They are like the guy who thinks he's really cool because he can beat the high score on the video game *Guitar Hero* but can't form a single chord on a real guitar. He has spent thousands of hours on a video game, pretending he can make music and can twang a bar and press a color-coated button in time to the beat, but he can't read a note of music or create a melody. I put these wannabe jumpers in three categories: Sideline Sitters, Constant Consumers, and Casual Clappers.

Sideline Sitters are critics who never affect people's lives but constantly complain to those who create. If their lips are moving, they are criticizing something. "That won't work." "The music was too loud." "We never do traditional hymns." "The sermon went too long." "Pastor Jeff was not funny today"—as if the pastor's sole job was to provide entertainment. And of course the jokes need to be wrapped up by 12:30 p.m. sharp.

The funny thing about critics is they never create anything. They never make anything happen. The most dangerous thing about Sideline Sitters is they never jump. Instead, they create doubt and fear around *your* pending decision to jump, all in an effort to keep you in your boat and preserve the status quo.

Constant Consumers are the guys who sit in church sucking up whatever is set before them as if there were nothing more to the Christian life than listening to sermons. They are the unproductive sloths who demand to consume a steady stream of songs, messages, books, and sermons. But even if they learn something, they never do anything with that knowledge. These people are dead branches that need to be trimmed.

Casual Clappers are the folks who say things like, "It's really super neat what you are doing." But in response to, "Hey, we could really use some help to care for these dying people," there is always an excuse as to why maybe next time will work. Get close enough to these people and you realize their favorite TV show or sporting event usually has priority over helping others or getting involved in anything. These people can be exposed by totaling up their combined time vegetating before the TV and comparing that with the time spent on the things of God. They approach God as they would a leisurely game of golf. Nothing really matters, and there certainly is no urgency.

Do any of these images describe you? Perhaps a little in each category?

TIME TO JUMP

One of my favorite Christmas stories is *A Christmas Carol* by Charles Dickens. There is a reason there have been twenty-one motion picture versions of this enduring story. Dickens's beloved story of Ebenezer Scrooge depicts a greedy miser who hates Christmas. Scrooge's dead business partner, Jacob Marley, returns as a ghost bound by the chains of his greed. Marley implores Scrooge not to make the same mistakes in life that he made. It was too late for him, but not yet too late for Scrooge.

Through visiting Christmases past, present, and future, Scrooge comes face-to-face with his own selfishness and greed, and it is ugly. He sees how the seeds of greed have reaped crops of loneliness and misery. Finally, after seeing visions of his own lonely funeral, Scrooge redeems his life and transforms into a caring, loving person.

Last Christmas, after watching *A Christmas Carol* for probably the thirty-fifth time, I wondered, *What if God, like the ghost of Christmas future, were to take me to my own funeral?* As I began to imagine what people might say or not say, it became a very powerful, even emotional thought.

Imagine that God transported you through time to attend your own funeral. There, standing at your funeral, you could see the impact of the things you did in your life. The difference you made in people's lives. People would be sharing about how you influenced their lives, how you were an inspiration and an example that pointed them toward God by the way you lived. Or not. But what if God took you one step further? What if God showed you not just Christmas future, but the Christmas that could have been? The life that could have been, should have been?

Here God would flash up scenes of each of our lives that never actually happened. These were the things God wanted to do with our lives, but we didn't let Him. If only we had decided to jump in and use the gifts He specifically gave us for those things we never did. God wanted to achieve great purposes through us. He wanted each of us to accomplish so much in the lives of others. But it never came to pass.

> The young girl I was supposed to talk to who committed suicide.
> The homeless woman who just needed a leg up and never got it.

The scores of children in Africa who were killed by
malaria for want of mosquito nets that I was supposed to
provide.
The friends who are lost because I was too scared to jump
into a spiritual conversation.

When faced with his ugly greed, Ebenezer Scrooge jumped.
Yes, even Scrooge became generous. What about you? Will you
have serious regrets at the end of your life because you were too
chained to your boat to jump?

Whenever I have a chance to speak to a sharp group of
businesspeople or young future leaders, I always leave them with
this challenge: "I'm not concerned that anyone in this group will
fail at anything. My concern is that you might succeed at something that didn't matter."

It is time for you to jump. No matter where you are in life, if
you're reading this, it's not too late.

*Lord, I do not want to succeed at something that doesn't matter. Expose the
comforts and securities that are preventing me from jumping. Please reveal
to me the amazing things You would have me accomplish for You. Give me
the wisdom to seize the opportunities to serve You in the areas where You
would have me serve. Amen.*

FIVE

Step It Up

I was about thirteen years old. My family was vacationing in the beautiful Hawaiian Islands with some family friends. Someone at our hotel told us about a local waterfall that had carved a smooth waterslide right into the rocks. We were up for the adventure, so we went to check it out.

The waterslide looked spectacular. As we made our way to the top of the rocks that formed the slide, I noticed a handful of local kids jumping off the rocks of the adjacent towering cliffs into the water. Whew, that looked scary.

After about an hour of fun on that wonderful natural slide (it's still the best waterslide I've ever been on in my life), we started eyeing the cliffs above and the local kids who were jumping. The kids in our group had a dare going to see if one of us would conjure up the guts to be the first mainlander to climb the cliff and do the jump. Seeing how I always wanted to beat the boys, I volunteered.

I made my way up the path cut into the rock wall. As I stepped up to the edge of the cliff, where the overhang suspended me thirty feet above the water, I began to seriously appreciate how high I really was. Basically I started to freak out. As much as I wanted to be the first California *girl* to jump, this was really too much. To make matters worse, it was windy . . . I stopped. It looked really far down. One of the younger boys in our group joined me on the cliff. Tim said, "If you're not going to jump, move over and I'll jump. Are you chicken?"

Before I could answer Tim's wisecrack, a local man, who must have been watching me for five minutes as I contemplated jumping, said, "Just step off."

"What?" I yelled.

"Just step off," he repeated.

"Yeah," Tim echoed. "Just step off."

Just taking a step seemed easy. I took steps all day long. *What's the big deal? It's just a step.* With that, I moved right to the edge, closed my eyes tight, and simply took a small step forward. My body instantly plunged into space and I free-fell with a scream of thrill all the way to the water. As I came up out of the water, feeling like a stunt girl on *Hawaii Five-0*, I yelled up to the boys, "What are you boys waiting for? Chickens! Just step off!"

I think I jumped off that cliff ten more times during our afternoon, but none of the other nine jumps was as thrilling as the first.

So what if you just can't jump? What if in your life with God you want to make a radical change but just can't? Some people are born jumpers. Others are more like I was, frozen on the edge of that Hawaiian cliff, unwilling to jump but willing to take a small step.

EVERY "DOING" STARTS WITH
A STEP, JUMP, OR LEAP

In his book *Love Does*, Bob Goff says, "Love is never stationary. In the end, love doesn't just keep thinking about it or keep planning for it. Simply put: love does."[1] Yes, first God is interested in your *love*. Then God is interested in what you are *doing*.

Throughout history God has prodded His people with questions to help us figure out what we are doing for Him.

In chapter 2, I described God's quiet call to Elijah. In 853 BC, in the midst of the craziness of freak winds, earthquakes, and fires, God quietly whispered a very simple question: *"What are you doing here, Elijah?"*

Nearly three millennia later, the same question was being asked of me as I sat in a little village on the shores of Lake Victoria, Uganda, Africa. *"What are you doing here, Shelene?"*

The question God asked Elijah was not for His benefit and certainly not for His information. God already knew the answer before He whispered the question. He had known even before Elijah was born and had designed that question to help Elijah come to grips with what he was going to *do*.

While sitting on the shores of Fishers Village, when I heard God's question in my mind, I did not at first recognize it as God's whispering voice. It was just my own restless thoughts—or so I thought. It was my own questioning, right? Wrong. With the persistence of that thought and with my discomfort and the stillness of my surroundings, I finally recognized that the quiet whisper in my thoughts was actually God's quiet voice of truth wanting to know what I was going to do with the information He had just disclosed to me.

God had designed that question—*"What are you doing here?"*—to help me come to grips with what I was going to *do*. He was gently prodding me to take my first step.

TAKING STEP ONE

Sometimes the decision to jump is scary, overwhelming, and paralyzing. Often we have a "deer in the headlights" response to the thought of jumping—we just freeze. Turning the corner from recognizing God's call to actually doing something involves an intermediate stage that many people never take. I like to call it *step one*.

God often requires us to take the first step of obedience before His supernatural power kicks in to accomplish through us what He chooses. But taking that first step of faith demonstrates our willingness to trust God, and He in turn will crown our efforts with His favor.

Throughout the Bible we see examples of God waiting for His people to take the first step of obedience before He intervened in miraculous ways:

> David had to first find the stones before God could use him to deliver Israel from Goliath.
> Moses' mother, Jochebed, had to first place baby Moses in the basket before God could use him to lead his people out of Egypt.
> Noah had to first start building an ark, never knowing if rain was going to come, before God could save his family from the Flood.
> Esther had to first risk her life to come before the king

before God stepped in and saved her people from genocide.

But there is not a more vivid example of the *step-one* principle than the story of Joshua.

God had promised the people of Israel a "land of milk and honey," but first He would have to deliver the evil city of Jericho into Israel's hand. The problem was that between Israel's army and their prize conquest was a massive natural barrier: the flooded river Jordan.

> Joshua told the people, "Consecrate yourselves, for tomorrow the LORD will do amazing things among you."
>
> Joshua said to the priests, "Take up the ark of the covenant and pass on ahead of the people." So they took it up and went ahead of them.
>
> And the LORD said to Joshua, "Today I will begin to exalt you in the eyes of all Israel, so they may know that I am with you as I was with Moses. Tell the priests who carry the ark of the covenant: 'When you reach the edge of the Jordan's waters, go and stand in the river.'" (Joshua 3:5–8)

What kind of plan was that? I can imagine that some of Joshua's trusted advisors would have advised against this "go stand in the river" plan. Here Joshua was—the new, untested leader of Israel. He was brand-new on the job, taking over after the death of the beloved, reliable, and trusted leader Moses. And his first big plan was to "go stand in the river"?

I can assure you this sounded crazy. What if it didn't work? He would look a fool having the nation's most powerful religious leaders stand humiliated in the middle of a flooded river, carrying the most sacred ark of God. This was an all-or-nothing step for Joshua. His credibility, his authority, and his influence as the nation's new leader were on the line.

> So when the people broke camp to cross the Jordan, the priests carrying the ark of the covenant went ahead of them. Now the Jordan is at flood stage all during harvest. Yet as soon as the priests who carried the ark reached the Jordan and their feet touched the water's edge, the water from upstream stopped flowing. It piled up in a heap a great distance away, at a town called Adam in the vicinity of Zarethan, while the water flowing down to the Sea of the Arabah (that is, the Dead Sea) was completely cut off. So the people crossed over opposite Jericho. The priests who carried the ark of the covenant of the LORD stopped in the middle of the Jordan and stood on dry ground, while all Israel passed by until the whole nation had completed the crossing on dry ground. (Joshua 3:14–17)

Israel's priests had to take the first step. A very literal first step. God required them to have faith in Him before all the people of Israel. "Go and stand in the river" were His explicit instructions. When in faith the priests took that step, the very instant their feet touched the waters of the Jordan, the Lord dammed up the waters. God came through.

WHAT'S STOPPING YOUR FIRST STEP?

Let me ask you a question: What must happen before you will jump?

Just because you may feel that God has called you to do something for Him does not necessarily mean you are ready to jump and do it. Most of us are reluctant to jump. So rather than a full jump, taking simply one step into the adventure He has put on your heart can get your momentum moving, and God will then empower your next step.

Thinking back to my cliff-jumping experience in Hawaii as a young teenager, taking that first little step was all I needed. Gravity took over from there, plunging me to where I wanted to go. Sometimes we need to just take a little step in our walk with God, trusting He will be our "gravity" and do the rest.

Reluctance to jump is the default human condition. We tend to love the status quo. This reality is perfectly illustrated by the fact that eleven disciples stayed in the boat and only one jumped out. So what was it about Peter that actually allowed him to overcome that natural reluctance to jump? In a word—faith. It is not enough just to believe God has the power to carry us through; we've got to take step one and get our feet wet.

FAITH FACILITATES TAKING STEP ONE

It was Peter's faith in Jesus' character that allowed Peter to take that leap out of the boat. He had done life with Jesus for several years. He saw the way Jesus lived and loved. He trusted Jesus because he had seen firsthand that Jesus was trustworthy. It was Peter's absolute confidence in Jesus' moral fiber that allowed him to take step one. When Jesus said, "Come," Peter had identified that it was Jesus who called, and he made a split-second decision to jump based on his entire experience with this man.

You may have participated in an exercise of faith that I call the "Faith Fall." My first experience with this exercise was at a youth group event when I was in high school. Our leader asked us to pair up with another person we trusted. Once we each found a partner, he instructed one person to stand behind the other, prepared to catch his partner before he hit the ground. Then he instructed the other partner to stand perfectly upright and while staying straight as a board, fall backward. Our partners were charged with the responsibility of catching us at the last possible second.

The success of this exercise depended wholly on the quality of the character of the partner each of us chose. Most were fortunate enough to choose a trustworthy person who would catch them before they hit the ground. Apparently my teenage judge of character wasn't so good, because the jokester I chose as a partner thought it would be funny to see me thump to the ground when at the last second he took a step away.

The great thing about God is He will never step away. The majestic, all-powerful, all-knowing God who sits on His throne is always faithful. Knowing His character, knowing His love and deep concern for us, knowing that He is trustworthy and always has our best interests in mind is so reassuring when we are on the verge of taking step one. And "the LORD makes firm the steps of the one who delights in him; though he may stumble, he will not fall, for the LORD upholds him with his hand" (Psalm 37:23–24).

The amazing trustworthiness of God is something we can count on in taking step one. You can be assured that the Lord will "make firm" your first step. When you make that first move, He will see to it that although you may stumble, you will not fall. He will be right there beside you with your hand in His.

Lord, help me recognize Your voice when You call. Help me recognize Your trustworthy character and trust that You have my best interests in mind. Burn into my heart the desire to do the tasks You want me to accomplish for You. Give me the strength and courage to take the first step toward what You want me to do. Please be there to finish with Your great power the tasks I have started and cannot complete without You. Amen.

SIX

Impossible Living

Recently I had a conversation with a friend of mine at my church. "Shelene, I feel like I am not really seeing or hearing God. He feels so far away."

From all I could see of this woman's life, she was the real thing. She loved God and she was busy serving in our church. She folded bulletins, set up chairs, and taught Sunday school every week.

Have you ever felt like that? Felt that you were not seeing God work? Felt that you couldn't hear God?

I have felt like that. I can remember praying and stopping and shouting to God, "Hello, God! Are You there?"

It's not an uncommon feeling for many Christians. We are involved in our churches. We sit in our pews and listen to some great sermons. We have highly talented musicians lead us in worship from the heart and are often genuinely touched by the music and praise.

What is the problem? Why do many Christians feel God is not showing Himself?

I believe too many Christians have been lulled, pacified, and numbed into the cradle of the modern "easy life." The effect of this has been that we don't need God. We don't really *need* Him to accomplish what we are doing.

We are not seeing God because in our self-created "Christianity Lite" world, we are not trying anything that only God can do. When was the last time you were in a situation that was impossible? For some of us, our lives are way too easy. We can't see God working because we are allergic to the impossible. We have designed our lives so that God never needs to step in. No wonder we can't see God. The fact is, He never really needs to show up.

Jesus spoke some profound words about a seemingly hopeless situation: "With man this is impossible, but not with God; all things are possible with God" (Mark 10:27).

Why do you think that verse is in the Bible? So we won't be inspired to attempt the impossible? Is the verse there because all things *aren't* really possible with God, and God was just trying to pull one over on us?

If we never try the impossible, God does not need to swoop in and save the day.

The Bible is full of examples of God's people attempting the impossible and God showing up big-time to save the day. One of my favorites is the often overlooked story of King Jehoshaphat's defeat of three massive armies that were marching to destroy Israel. These enemies of the Israelites were bent on their destruction—taking their lands and carrying off their wives and children. The Bible says, "Some people came and told Jehoshaphat, 'A vast army is coming against you from Edom, from the other side of the Dead Sea' . . . Alarmed, Jehoshaphat resolved to inquire of the LORD, and he proclaimed a fast for all Judah" (2 Chronicles 20:2–3).

Israel was facing impossible odds. Its military strength at the time could not have defeated one of these armies, let alone the combined strength of three. Jehoshaphat knew the condition of Israel's army; he knew how desperate the situation was, so he turned in prayer and fasting to God, begging Him to do the impossible and provide salvation for his land.

God had a plan. Unknown to his enemies, Jehoshaphat had a top secret force of handpicked specialized military operatives. He would deploy this powerful force out in front of the main army. These men were going to be used by God to do the impossible. The king himself specifically appointed them for their skill and training. Yes, they were picked for their fine ability . . . to sing.

What? *Sing?* Yes, sing.

> After consulting the people, Jehoshaphat appointed men to sing to the LORD and to praise him for the splendor of his holiness as they went out at the head of the army, saying: "Give thanks to the LORD, for his love endures forever."
>
> As they began to sing and praise, the LORD set ambushes against the men of Ammon and Moab and Mount Seir who were invading Judah, and they were defeated. The Ammonites and Moabites rose up against the men from Mount Seir to destroy and annihilate them. After they finished slaughtering the men from Seir, they helped to destroy one another.
>
> When the men of Judah came to the place that overlooks the desert and looked toward the vast army, they saw only dead bodies lying on the ground; no one had escaped. (2 Chronicles 20:21–24)

Jehoshaphat was absolutely out of his comfort zone. Because of that, he was able to see God really show up.

I never feel the presence of God more than when I am completely out of my comfort zone. Sometimes comfort and safety are like a repellent to seeing God at work. Sadly, I was a Christian dedicated to living my life to maximize my personal ease and security, and consequently I never put myself in a position to see God perform the miracles He might have. When it comes to serving God, most of us never take a single risk, and certainly never get out of our comfort zones.

So, what are you doing in your life right now that you could not do without the power of almighty God? If you can't answer that, there is a good chance you feel distant from Him. However, the converse is also true. If you can rattle off a list of things you are doing right now that would be impossible without God's intervention, I will bet that God is very real and is showing His hand constantly in your life.

If you had trouble thinking of an answer to the question, now is the time to jump. You need to make some changes, start doing the impossible, and give God a chance to show up in your life in a miraculous way.

DISCOMFORT IN ATLANTA

It was March 11, 2005, when a man named Brian Nichols, who was on trial for rape in Atlanta, Georgia, terrorized the entire city with a killing spree that started in a Fulton County courthouse when he overpowered the deputy escorting him into court. He proceeded to hunt down and kill the judge presiding over his case. After killing three other people who tried to stop him, he escaped the courthouse and touched off the largest manhunt in Georgia history. Nichols avoided capture for more than twenty-four hours, shooting anyone who got in his way, until he crossed paths with Ashley Smith, a brave young single mom who was struggling to find God.

It was about 2:00 a.m. on March 12. Ashley had just pulled into the parking lot of her apartment complex. She was walking from her car to her front door when she realized someone had come up behind her. She started to scream when Nichols stuck a gun in her side and said in a hushed tone, "Don't scream. If you don't scream, I won't hurt you." Nichols forced his way into her apartment and then tied her up with duct tape and an extension cord, and wrapped her with a curtain. He then carried her into the bathroom and placed her on a stool.

As Ashley sat on that stool, tied up by a man who had just brutally killed four people, waiting for her fate while he took a shower, things looked about as impossible as they could get.

After she gained Nichols's trust, he unbound her.

We went to my room. And I asked him if I could read. He said, "What do you want to read?" "Well, I have a book in my room." So I went and got it. I got my Bible. And I got a book called "The Purpose-Driven Life." I turned it to the chapter that I was on that day. It was Chapter 33. And I started to read the first paragraph of it. After I read it, he said, "Stop, will you read it again?" I said, "Yeah. I'll read it again." So I read it again to him.[1]

On Day 33 of *The Purpose Driven Life*, author Rick Warren says, "We serve God by serving others. The world defines greatness in terms of power, possessions, prestige, and position. If you can demand service from others, you have arrived. In our self-serving culture with its *me-first* mentality, acting like a servant is not a popular concept."[2]

And I asked him what he thought. And he said, "I think it was to talk to people and tell them about you." He needed hope for his life. He told me that he was already dead. He said, "Look at me, look at my eyes. I am already dead."

And I said, "You are not dead. You are standing right in front of me. If you want to die, you can. It's your choice."

But after I started to read to him, he saw, I guess he saw my faith and what I really believed in. And I told him I was a child of God and that I wanted to do God's will. I guess he began to want to. That's what I think.

And he was hungry, so I cooked him breakfast. He was overwhelmed with—"Wow," he said, "real butter, pancakes?"

And I just talked with him a little more, just about, about, we pretty much talked about God . . . what his reason was, why he made it out of there.

I said, "Do you believe in miracles? Because if you don't believe in miracles, you are here for a reason. You're here in my apartment for some reason. You got out of that courthouse with police everywhere, and you don't think that's a miracle? You don't think you're supposed to be sitting here right in front of me listening to me tell you, you know, your reason here?"

I said, "You know, your miracle could be that you need to, you need to be caught for this. You need to go to prison and you need to share the Word of God with them, with all the prisoners there."[3]

At about 9:30 a.m., Nichols let Ashley leave to pick up her daughter. When she reached the first stop sign, she dialed 911. Within minutes a SWAT team surrounded Ashley's apartment with Nichols inside. Within a short time, Brian Nichols freely gave himself up by waving a piece of white cloth in surrender. He is now serving a life sentence for his crimes.

Do you think Ashley's situation was impossible? If I was a betting girl, just as I would have bet against Jehoshaphat and all Israel escaping three marching armies, I would have bet against Ashley coming out of that apartment alive. An accused rapist who had just murdered four people in cold blood had her bound hand and foot. Can you say "impossible situation"?

She did not need to read *The Purpose Driven Life* to this murderer. That was certainly not the safe thing to do. She did not need to put her life in further danger by challenging what this guy was doing. She chose to share the only thing that really mattered in that impossible situation. She read a book about pursuing a relationship with God.

What about you? Are you tired of not seeing God at work? Are you playing it safe in your service for God? It just might be time to throw caution to the wind and get a little uncomfortable. Then watch how God shows up to help you do the impossible.

Lord, give me the courage to become uncomfortable and try the impossible. Give me the faith to see the impossible transform to the possible with Your help. And give me the opportunities to live out my faith in a way that is worthy of the position You have given to me. Amen.

SEVEN

A New Christmas Miracle

I had returned from Africa about mid-November, and as I was unpacking some lingering items in my oversized suitcase and placing them in a storage closet, I came across a box that had several Christmas gifts from the year before, unwrapped but still in the product packaging. Although we had spent hundreds of dollars on these gifts, they were so unnecessary they had managed not to get touched in almost an entire year. It about made me sick.

I had just left a village where kids were starving to death, and I had personally witnessed how far a little help could go to save a child's life, and here I was, face-to-face with the reality of my excess. I had so much excess that the gifts that had seemed so important eleven and a half months earlier were rotting in my closet.

What if I had simply donated the two hundred dollars we had spent on these superfluous gifts we did not need and never used? How many kids would still be alive? I thought of all the toys my kids had loved on Christmas Day but were seldom used within days and thrown in the trash within months.

Christmas was fast approaching, and I had just been hit in

the face with the sobering reality of my wastefulness. Worse yet, up until my trip to Uganda, Christmas was all about me. What I wanted, what I would get, *my* gifts, *my* kids, *my* family, decorating *my* house, and eating *my* yummy food. After I got back from Africa, that egocentric, narcissistic, self-centered view of Christmas felt very wrong.

I resolved this Christmas was going to be different. I was not going to buy into the materialism, waste, and debt that happened every year. Besides . . . it isn't my birthday. It's Jesus' birthday! I spoke with my husband and little sister, Shanda, about my idea of doing something completely different this Christmas, and they agreed.

I started calling around and remembered a friend, Tina, who was a neonatal care nurse at Children's Hospital in Los Angeles. I contacted her and asked if there was a deserving family of a sick child on whom our family could bestow gifts at Christmas. She said yes, actually, there was. After getting the family's permission, my friend explained, "We have a patient we call Baby Miracle. She is only five months old and has never been out of the hospital. By almost every estimate she should not be here. She has several failing organs, and it will probably only be a matter of months."

Tina went on to explain that Baby Miracle's mother had several children and took the bus back and forth to the hospital to visit her little fighting Miracle. I requested the names and ages of all the kids. "We'd like to bless them this Christmas, buy them gifts, and come visit them Christmas morning at the hospital."

"Christmas morning?" Tina asked with surprise.

"Yes, we're making some changes, and it's about time Christmas is about somebody besides me."

Tina promised she would take care of the approvals and set everything up. I hung up the phone. *"Yes!"* I shouted while simultaneously doing a fist pump.

I immediately called my sister and invited her family over for dinner to share the news about our upcoming Christmas adventure.

That night Shanda and her family came over, and I shared my conversation with Nurse Tina with everyone over dinner. I had waited all day to explain what we were going to do this Christmas; I could barely contain my excitement. Between bites of chili and Grands biscuits, I explained the idea of all of us forgoing a Christmas gift for the sake of someone else who was in real need. Blake, Brooke, and my nieces, Maddie and Saige, professed to love the idea, but I was not wholly convinced they were fully on board until Shanda and I gave the kids the money that normally would have been used for their gifts.

Once dinner was over, we all piled into the SUV and drove to the mall to shop for Baby Miracle and her family. The dads and Blake decided it would be wise to stay out of the way of girls in the mall, so they suggested we split up: boys shop for boys and girls shop for girls. We agreed to meet back in two hours. Blake, who normally would prefer to have shards of glass sprinkled in his eyes to shopping at a mall, was actually excited to go to the sporting goods store in search of some football gear he knew Baby Miracle's brother would love.

As Jesus' birthday grew closer and closer, the excitement over the celebration of the birth of our Savior grew stronger and stronger. Our Christmas Eve service never felt more right knowing that instead of waking up to gifts under our tree, we were waking up to a Happy Birthday Jesus party. Please don't misunderstand; our kids still received gifts. They got gifts from grandparents, aunts, uncles, and friends. But Brice and I only gave them a stocking of necessities. Many kids in America want for nothing, including ours. I wanted our kids to learn that the gift belongs to the giver. Up until now I had been failing at teaching that.

As Christmas morning arrived, we all woke with an excitement and a joy that was strangely different. On the car ride to the hospital, we were met with an avalanche of questions, including, "Is Baby Miracle going to live?" (How to answer that question from a five-year-old? Particularly when everything I had been told pointed to Baby Miracle's imminent passing?)

"Uh, I don't know, honey. We are just gonna have to see."

"Can I hold her?" Brooke inquired.

"Uh, I don't know, honey. We are just gonna have to see."

"Will the mommy be there with Baby Miracle?" Blake asked.

"Uh, I don't know, honey. We are just gonna have to see." Geesh! I sure didn't seem to know much.

As we arrived at Children's Hospital, we wound our way several stories deep into the underground parking structure. Once parked, we unpacked the mountain of gifts we had purchased, wrapped, and stashed in the backs of our SUVs. Footballs, basketballs, Nerf guns, sweat suits, socks, Nike jackets, Hello Kitty backpacks, mittens, Polly Pockets, a giant, fuzzy stuffed bear for Baby Miracle, and gift cards and prepaid credit cards for her mom. As we looked up at the gigantic six-story hospital, I couldn't help but blurt out, "Wow! This place is *huge*!"

As we entered the lobby we approached the visitors' check-in and there were four enormous, refrigerator-size cardboard boxes overflowing with toys that had been dropped off for the sick children. It struck me that on that Christmas morning, the lobby was filled with stuffed animals for the kids, but (except for our family) not a single person was there. The place was a virtual ghost town.

We were greeted by a security guard, who seemed surprised to see us, but then seeing the packages we were carrying, pointed to the four stuffed cardboard toy boxes and said, "Toy drop-offs there."

"Oh, no. We are here to visit a child."

"No, ma'am. You can't give toys directly to the children. You can only drop them off here."

It took a few minutes to convince Mr. Mall Cop that we were really there to visit a child and someone way above his pay grade had preapproved it. Eventually the well-meaning security guard relented and we signed in, were given wristbands, and were escorted to the neonatal care unit on the sixth floor East. When the elevator doors opened, we were greeted with a *swoosh* of cold hospital air and peered out to see shiny polished floors and a surplus of assorted scary-looking medical contraptions lining the hallways.

After taking a few deep breaths to calm our nerves before stepping out of the elevator, we bounced into the unit, wishing everyone we saw a "Merry Christmas!" and passing out Santa hats and candy canes. We gave a big box of See's candy and a giant can of Almond Roca to the nurses and thanked them for loving the sick children.

Tina greeted us at the main nurses station and walked with

us to Baby Miracle's room. There she was, sitting upright in her hospital bed. She looked like the most beautiful doll we had ever seen. Our kids quickly gathered around her bed and wished her a merry Christmas. Baby Miracle's mom was not yet there, but her fifteen-year-old sister sat by her side.

Our kids started singing and dancing around her bed with a performance they had given at their school Christmas program a few days before. As the kids performed a funny little Jamaican Christmas song that goes, "Aye, mon, what are you lookin' for up in the sky?" Baby Miracle smiled and clapped and seemed to enjoy every minute of it. Afterward, we gave Baby Miracle's sister her Christmas gifts, as well as the gifts for her siblings and mother. Then we walked the floor and visited all the children who were stuck in the hospital that Christmas morning, singing Christmas carols with them.

Jesus said, "It is more blessed to give than to receive" (Acts 20:35). We have all heard that verse. We even marginally, half-heartedly believe it, but most of us don't live it. Not really, not in a way that would convince an unbiased bystander who was watching.

On our drive back home to meet the rest of our extended family for Christmas dinner, we were excited to share the stories of the people we had met. The kids unanimously voiced that skipping a Christmas gift for the sake of someone else was not nearly as bad as it had first sounded. No one had regrets. Instead, the kids kept asking, "Can we do this next year?" "Can we go back and visit Baby Miracle?" *Yes*, of course.

That Christmas night, *"It is better to give than receive"* rang true in our home. And it has every Christmas since.

Lord, help me take my eyes off my comforts and myself so I might be an encouragement to those who need inspiration. Give me the strength to live a life that is about something more than my never-ending wants. Help me learn to skip the excesses of my culture to help those in need. Amen.

EIGHT

Every Jump Ripples

If our Christmas story stopped there, it would be good, right? But it doesn't. God really wanted to press hard on my heart that skipping self and serving others was how our family was to celebrate Christmas every year.

A friend of mine, Todd Ross, said to me one day, "Shelene, you live life for God and make ripples happen." *Ripples* are defined as "a small wave or series of gentle waves across a surface."[1] We have all seen ripples moving in concentric circles away from the splash of a stone thrown into a lake or pond. In the same way, ripples happen when we say yes to God and do whatever it is He wants us to do. Our little splash has a reverberating effect on others.

The apostle Paul recognized the incredible effect our obedience to God can have on others. It's more than synergistic when you make the decision to jump; it's a supernatural splash of God's incredible love rippling to those around you. I love how *The Message* translation of Paul's words emphasizes how God's love can so fill our hearts that it splashes over onto everyone we come in contact with: "And may the Master pour on the love so it fills your lives and splashes over on everyone around you, just as it does from us to you" (1 Thessalonians 3:12).

God was in the process of teaching me that every jump I made caused a ripple in the life of someone else.

As the Christmas season came to an end and the New Year rolled in, I received a call from my friend Tina from Children's Hospital. The moment I heard her voice, I thanked her profusely and expressed what an unforgettable time we all had on Christmas morning.

She then explained, "A nurse named Rachel who was working on Christmas asked me why your family came on Christmas morning. She wanted to know why you brought all those gifts for people you did not even know. I told her, 'To celebrate Jesus' birthday.' I then told her about you and your trip to Africa. She was shocked, saying, 'That's where my heritage is from, and I've never even been to Uganda.'"

"Tina," I said, "tell her I am leaving in June to go back to Uganda. She should come. And, Tina, you should come too. You and Rachel would be like doctors over there."

"Let me check with Rachel and get back to you. But, Shelene . . . I'm in."

"Shut *up*! This would be awesome!" I said, remembering all the children I had helplessly left who so desperately needed medical care. I hung up the phone and just knew that these girls were going to accompany me back to Uganda.

All because I got out of bed on Christmas morning and got a little uncomfortable—wow! Ripples really do happen. Sure enough, both Tina and Rachel said *yes* and made plans to accompany me back to Africa. Children's Hospital donated medicine so they could deworm entire villages of people. Another reminder that every jump ripples.

As our June trip started getting closer, God had still another stranger He was going to add to the mix. My family and I were eating lunch at a restaurant in our neighborhood. We were sitting at a table on an outdoor patio with a large water fountain that had become a collection receptacle for an assortment of coins tossed in exchange for wishes. As our kids were running around the fountain and throwing in pennies, another family was sitting just a few tables away. Their kids were also dancing around the fountain. The mother called out to her daughter, "Brooke!"

I immediately turned around because that's my daughter's name. Smiling at the young mom, I said, "Hi. Our daughter's named Brooke too. Brooke meet Brooke." And we all stood up and greeted each other.

As Brice and I began to talk with our new friends, Jade and Stephanie, I remembered that I had a Uganda information meeting scheduled at our house. I quickly shared that I was going to Africa and had a few people coming over in an hour and needed to run. Stephanie blurted out, "Oh my gosh, I've always wanted to go to Africa and help the poor!"

"Well then, you need to come to this meeting."

Stephanie looked guiltily at her husband and the three small kids grabbing at their daddy's legs. With a wink and a nod, Jade said, "I've got the kids, babe. Go to the meeting." I quickly gave Stephanie our address, and just like that we had another traveler willing to say *yes* to God.

June arrived before we knew it. Our team of ten (including nurses Tina and Rachel and my new friend Stephanie) met up at Los Angeles International Airport (LAX) for that fantastic flight in coach to Entebbe, Uganda. I was sincerely excited to unplug from everything and spend ten days with God. When

I'm in Uganda, I can just breathe. People aren't uptight if I don't return their texts or e-mails or calls right away. They understand—I'm in Africa!

Other than cramped legs and sore butts, our team made it safe and sound to Entebbe, and we tolerated the bouncy bus ride to Gaba. There we were greeted by a group of ladies from Gaba Community Church and by the big brilliant smile of Pastor Peter. Bethany Village was our next destination, and I began to warn the team about the wooden boats and the Mr. Universe disembarking experience. Suddenly several speedboats pulled up to the shore.

"Pastor Peter, when did you get these speedboats?"

"You got these, Mamma Shelene."

"No, Pastor, I think you have me confused with another *muzunga*."

"No, Mamma Shelene. You'll see."

I was thinking Pastor Peter had lost his mind, but before I could let my mind wander too much, the normally thirty-minute wooden-boat ride was almost over—it was now ten minutes. As the new speedboats whipped around the bend to Bethany Village, I saw a wonderful sight. There on the shore, where previously only grass and a couple of fitness-model types had once stood, was a beautiful sight—a large wooden dock rising out of the water! The speedboats pulled up to the dock, and we were thrilled to avoid being thrown over the shoulder of Mr. Universe and instead stepped out onto the dock's wooden deck.

"*Wow*, Pastor. I love it!"

Then, with a pearly-white smile, Peter explained, "When you gave me the money to build the dock, another man said, 'Well then, you are going to need some boats,' and God gave us some speedboats."

The more I see God at work, the more I understand that saying *yes* to God makes ripples. Pastor Peter could have pocketed that four hundred dollars. He didn't know if I'd ever be back, and for that matter, I didn't think I'd ever be back to Uganda. Pastor Peter was faithful with little. The Bible says, "He who is faithful with little will be faithful with much" (Luke 16:10, paraphrased).

Until my first trip to Uganda, I always thought that verse was talking about money. Now I realize it can also mean much more. I had information about this place, and I was now responsible for what I saw here in Africa. I know that I don't have the power to save the world; that's God's job. But I can leave each place I visit a little better than it was when I arrived.

As we all walked off the dock and headed over to Fishers Village, my heart started to beat rapidly. My last memory of that place was the time I had heard God's quiet whisper. That sweet, smiling, hungry boy who had been playing in front of me—was he going to be dead?

As I prepared my heart for the worst, Fred, our interpreter from the last trip, walked up to me as if he could read my mind and said, "Mamma Shelene, the little boy you met last time in Fisher Village?"

"Yes," I said with anxious anticipation in my voice.

"Well, he is hungry no more."

Really? I thought. My heart leapt. My brain was racing faster than my mouth could talk (a rarity for me). *Wow! There must have been a doctor or someone who came in after me, just like the man with the speedboats, and helped this young boy.*

I never said a word because the interpreter continued his sentence by saying with a smile, "Yes, he's in heaven, with Jesus."

Here I had wanted to save him, when God was ready to

deliver this boy into His arms. I am grateful for the confidence I have that I will see him again one day.

Sometimes we get so focused on our one- or five-year plans that we forget God has a two-hundred-plus-year plan for each of us. Our life on planet Earth is only a vapor, and we will exit here. May this sweet little boy's life remind me to set my heart on things above, not on earthly things.

There I was, standing once again in Fishers Village. So much had happened in my life in the six months since I had been there. So much had changed. I had said *yes* to bikes, *yes* to getting my eyes off myself, and my whole self-centered perspective had changed. I had said *yes* to the Lord's whispering voice and challenged others to join me.

Standing there on the dirt path leading up the center of the village, I took in the reaction of the team witnessing Fishers Village for the first time. I spotted Tina and Rachel opening up their backpacks and giving out the life-saving medicine they'd brought to rid the villagers of worms. Others were playing games and loving on the kids and families.

Sometime later, Rachel began treating a beautiful five-year-old girl named Angela. As Rachel lifted up Angela's tattered, muddy dress, I saw alarm on her face. Tina and I rushed over to help Rachel, and I asked what was wrong. I am not in the medical field, but what I saw was distressing. Angela had a gruesome infestation of worms circling under her skin. Swollen, bloody, bruised baby skin was teeming with worms. Some were boring holes right through her skin, trying to exit her body. I gasped and shrank back in shock.

Rachel and Tina were the consummate professionals. Opening

their backpacks and tending to Angela was second nature to these well-skilled nurses; this was real-life *Grey's Anatomy*. Rachel then announced, "This girl needs a doctor ASAP. She needs serious medical attention."

"Where are Angela's parents?" she continued. "We need to take her across Lake Victoria to the medical center at Gaba Community Church immediately."

Our interpreter quickly discovered that both of Angela's parents were dead, but he found the girl's uncle, and soon we had permission to take her to Gaba. Rachel and Tina loaded her onto the speedboat and zoomed back across the lake to the recently completed Wentz Medical Center.

As the doctor started examining her, he noticed something troubling with her heartbeat. "She needs to be taken to the hospital in Kampala," he said.

Without delay, Rachel jumped into a van from Gaba church and headed to the hospital in Kampala with the girl. The hospital doctors quickly diagnosed that the little girl needed immediate surgery or she would die. Without hesitation, as if Rachel had given birth to the child herself, Rachel said, "Yes . . . do it. Whatever it takes, whatever it costs." And just like that, the girl's life was saved.

Love makes you say *yes*. That kind of love is heroic.

Rachel became Angela's sponsor. The child was able to heal and soon started attending Bethany School in Gaba.

Every jump ripples. Had my family not gotten out of the house on Christmas morning and decided to say yes and serve others, we would have never met Rachel, and she would have never come to Uganda, and little Angela would have never had a chance. She would have died.

Not long after returning from Uganda, I received a phone call from a friend from my church. She was upset and told me that Jen and Steve Hall's ten-year-old son, Logan, had just been airlifted to Children's Hospital. The Halls were a dear church family, and Jen was a good friend of mine. They didn't know what was wrong, but a group from the church was heading down to the hospital to pray in the lobby.

I felt compelled to go and made the forty-five-minute drive from my house to the hospital. I found a crowd of seventy-five people gathered in the lobby to support Logan and his family. We broke up into three groups to pray together.

Just as we finished praying, Jen and Steve came out of the elevators. Jen asked if I'd go up to Logan's room and pray. As I stepped off the elevator, a familiar scene greeted me. I had just been in these halls on Christmas Day, visiting Baby Miracle. And guess who was there? That's right, Tina, the pediatric nurse who just months earlier had been with me to Africa.

I entered Logan's room, and there, lying on a hospital bed, with no shirt on, was a healthy-looking boy. Through her tears, Jen told me that Logan and his friend had gone for a bike ride, after which they had gone swimming, had a little dinner, and then started riding their bikes again around the court in front of Logan's home.

Suddenly Logan's friend ran into the house and shouted, "Mrs. Hall, Logan needs his dad!"

He hadn't crashed. He'd just set his bike down in the street and collapsed. Steve, a fireman trained as a paramedic, was there within minutes, working to revive his son. Not wanting to waste time waiting for an ambulance when Logan was unresponsive, a neighbor, Steve, sister Ali, and brother Jake accompanied Logan as they drove to the local hospital. Ali sang to Logan during the entire car ride.

Later, when things did not improve, a medevac helicopter rushed Logan to Children's Hospital Los Angeles. He had suffered from a massive hemorrhaging of the brain. Following brain surgery, he had experienced multiple devastating strokes. Despite our prayers over the next few weeks, Logan never woke up again. We were all devastated by the loss of this young light. Although the Halls were comforted by the knowledge that Logan was in heaven, the reality of the long separation before they would see him again was a painful burden to endure.

When Logan died, the Halls decided to donate their son's organs to give life to another child whose organs were failing and desperately needed a transplant.

Guess who some of those organs went to? Yup, you guessed it: the little baby our family had visited and prayed for back on Christmas morning, Baby Miracle. You see, every jump ripples.

Saying *yes* to God is an adventure, and if we fail to say *yes*, there are things He wants to show us and let us experience that we will miss. Saying yes to God risks that things will get a little uncomfortable, but the end result will be worth it.

A *yes* to God is motivated by a heart of love. The yes from me and my family to get uncomfortable that Christmas morning; the yes from nurse Tina and nurse Rachel to go to Uganda; the yes from Jade Molina to encourage his wife to join our team;

the yes from the man who bought the speedboats; and the yes from the Halls to donate their son's organs *all* came from hearts of love.

Love motivates us to jump and the consequences ripple out to everyone around us. Say *yes* and love someone. Say *yes* and jump. Then enjoy the ripples you get to see because you were faithful to God's call.

Lord, give me the wisdom to see the things You are asking me to do. Make my heart willing to give You a yes even when I am scared and uncomfortable. Give me the strength to live my life in such a way that others are inspired to follow hard after You. Use the ripples from my life to draw others closer to You. And remind me every day that my life is just a vapor. Amen.

NINE

The Fear Factor

The moment I said yes to my pastor's request, I was gripped with fear. *What did I get myself into?* Our pastor, Francis Chan, had just asked me to do something that in my mind was totally and completely crazy, and I, for some unknown reason, had in fact accepted his request.

Francis had asked me to be in charge of a community barbecue our church was having in partnership with an inner-city ministry in South Central Los Angeles, far away from the safety of my little suburban community. The setting for this barbecue would be 2.1 miles from the starting place and epicenter of the 1992 Los Angeles riots following the Rodney King verdict that some in the community viewed as a racially motivated injustice.

Why was I so gripped with fear? Well, obsessive safety had been ingrained in my head since I was a child.

I was raised by a street-smart, safety-first kind of dad. He was a reserve police officer and a sniper for the department's SWAT team. He chose to raise our family in a bedroom suburb of Los Angeles whose crime rate was the lowest in the nation. Safety and security were a really big deal in our family.

As kids, my little sister and I were put through intensive

emergency training sessions. While training for fire safety, we had the joy of crawling out of our second-story bedroom windows onto a patio cover and jumping into our pool, all to prepare us "just in case there's a fire."

To test us on neighborhood safety, strange men in cars followed us on the short walk up the street to our elementary school. They were actually fellow police officers my dad had tasked with scaring us to see how we would react.

When I first started driving, my father had specifically instructed me to "never, under any circumstances" get off the freeway at Vermont Street in L.A. We were forbidden to go into this "dangerous" area of South Central Los Angeles.

Now here I was, not only driving into this neighborhood, but planning to spend quite a bit of time in the forbidden zone, preparing for the upcoming barbecue and kids carnival.

Francis Chan sums up my misgivings—and the solution— best in this excerpt from his book *Crazy Love*:

> We are consumed by safety and comfort. Obsessed with it, actually . . . We've made safety our highest priority. We've elevated safety to the neglect of whatever God's best is, whatever would bring God the most glory, or whatever would accomplish His purposes in our lives and in the world . . . People who are obsessed with Jesus aren't consumed with their personal safety and comfort above all else. Obsessed people care more about God's kingdom coming to this earth than their own lives being shielded from pain or distress.[1]

Those words were easier to read on the pages of *Crazy Love* than to live out.

We needed a site visit, so I managed to convince my best friend and Hollywood talent agent Barbara Cameron to go with me. Barbara is best known to the public as mother to child stars Kirk Cameron (*Growing Pains*) and Candace Cameron (*Full House*). We headed into the forbidden neighborhood in my black SUV to scout out the location for the barbecue.

While driving down to the site, I told Barbara about this crazy couple who were meeting us at their house in the forbidden neighborhood.

I explained that I had never met Richard and Shelly Brown, but Francis had told me about this young accountant and his wife who had decided to make a radical life change. Richard had been a successful auditor at the accounting firm of Ernst & Young in beautiful Irvine, California. After hearing the founder of World Impact (an inner-city missions organization) speak at their church's mission conference, the plight of the inner-city youth weighed heavily on Richard's heart. After careful consideration, the Browns left their Orange County apartment, Richard left his high-paying accounting job, and they moved to South Central Los Angeles to help the urban poor.

"Really?" Barbara said. "What would make someone want to do that?"

"I'm not sure, but I can't wait to meet them."

As Barbara and I were looking for the address of this crazy couple, I missed my turn and found myself going down the wrong street. It was unquestionably the wrong street. The area looked like something out of a war zone, with graffiti on the walls of houses and fences, doors dangling off hinges, broken windows, and peeling paint on most of the run-down homes.

Cars sporting bullet holes from drive-by shootings were parked haphazardly on dead brown grass in the front yards.

As my SUV proceeded down the street, to the right and partly in the street, we were approaching what looked like three big, good-looking young men washing a car. As we passed by, they all, in sync, stopped what they were doing and stared at us as our blond hair blew in the wind out our open windows and sunroof.

I slapped a huge, nervous smile on my face and waved. One of the three nodded and waved back with a smirk on his face, while the other two just glared. Once we'd passed, they continued with their work, vigorously washing their car.

I looked at Barbara, who now had gone completely silent (and appeared somewhat pale). "See, Barb? It's not that bad down here. Those guys were even out washing their car."

She scowled back at me. "Buddy, those guys weren't washing their car; they were stripping somebody's car."

"What?" I said, at the same instant realizing the boys had not been washing the wheels but unbolting and stealing them instead.

"In broad daylight, at 11:00 a.m., no less. Well, they certainly are brave."

She looked at me. "Who is going to stop them?"

"Good point, Barb."

After a few more turns, I finally found the street of the ex–Orange County couple and headed down it. Their street was a collection of seventy-year-old homes with security bars on the doors and windows.

We pulled up to the curb in front of the address we had been given. Barbara and I exchanged nervous glances as we got out of my SUV and walked up to the front door. All the while, I kept looking back at my car, half expecting somebody to jump out of the bushes and make off with my polished aluminum wheels.

I was feeling anxious as we knocked on the door of the Browns' home. When the door opened, I was shocked to see a woman not all that different from me standing in the doorway. This was not what I had expected. Where was the homely brown missionary dress and straggly graying hair piled in a bun?

Despite the undoubtedly surprised looks on our faces, she introduced herself as Shelly Brown and kindly invited us into their home, which also sported bars on the windows.

Once inside, Shelly got us some water and then shared how she had been unsure at first about moving to South Central Los Angeles.

She showed us the bullet holes in her windows. After examining the bullet holes, I could understand why she was reluctant to move here. I thought, *I'm with ya, girl. I would have come kicking and screaming.* But for once, I kept my thoughts to myself.

A short time later, Richard came home, and I was again bewildered. He seemed to be a totally normal, sharp guy. Before meeting him I had been thinking this guy must have been laid off or made a few bad investments, lost all his clients' money, and then decided he'd move to L.A. and become a World Impact missionary.

This couple was good looking and hip. Yet here they were, in a seriously rough neighborhood.

Shelly explained how her initial reluctance had grown into a deep love for their community. Then Richard offered to take us up the street to the school that would make a great venue for the community barbecue and carnival. Excited and anxious to get out of there before dark, we piled into my car and headed down the street.

We pulled up to the school, and I began to share my ideas for the community barbecue with him. "Look," I said, "I'm not interested in coming down here to serve with a better-than-thou attitude. But if you will allow us to do this barbecue as if I were putting it on in my own backyard, then I'm your girl."

"What do you mean?" he asked.

"I mean, I'm thinking about putting out tables and chairs, linens, decorations, and catering by a popular barbecue restaurant so we can sit down and dine with the community. I want to get to know them and hear their stories and share mine." I went on to explain that we'd do a complete carnival for the kids, with game booths, face painting, ball toss, and a football throw. We'd give away prizes, gift cards—the works.

Richard loved the idea, and the school was the perfect venue. Richard offered to have his team invite the city officials, arrange for a huge fire truck, and line up some bounce houses for the kids.

We all agreed to proceed, said our good-byes, and Barbara and I hopped back into my car and headed home.

———

As the barbeque quickly approached, I held several meetings at our home to plan and prepare for the event. We had a good crew ready to make it happen. I checked in with Francis and gave him an update.

But on the morning of the event, fear gripped me again. Up until then, I had been so busy planning that I'd forgotten how dangerous the area was.

We arrived at the venue, and Barbara got going on what she does best: decorating. She had decided on a red, white, and blue theme. We put out the tablecloths, baskets of red apples for centerpieces, and red and blue balloons tied to the basket handles, flying high for all to see. Our team got the carnival set up.

The caterer, Red's Barbecue, was ready to go. The fire truck arrived and city officials began to show up. We had all the gift cards, prizes, DVDs, and CDs we would need. Only one thing was missing: people. As our team anxiously waited, I noticed a man walking up to the perimeter fence of the school. He paced back and forth, eyeing everything, like a mountain lion ready to pounce. I called out to him, "Hi. Get your family and come on in. It's free."

"I know that," he called back, "but you better quit flying those gang colors right now!"

"What?" I said.

He must have been able to tell I had no idea what he was talking about. He pointed at our crimson red and dark blue balloons flying overhead.

"Your balloons . . . you're flying gang colors."

"Oh, got it," I said. Then I shouted to Barbara and anyone else who would listen, "Pop the balloons! Pop the balloons *now*!"

Before you could blink, the balloons were gone.

At this point it was forty minutes past the scheduled time of our event. I was beginning to lose hope. A few more men paced the perimeter of the chain-link fence and then left. It was killing me. *Don't they smell the delicious barbeque tri-tip and chicken? We have it all: barbecued pleasures, yummy rolls, loaded baked potatoes, with award-winning beans and killer desserts.*

Then it happened. Sure enough, before I could announce

this thing was a bust and order our team to pack everything up, waves of people by the hundreds started walking down the street toward the school. As the families entered the gate, our team greeted them with smiles. We escorted the kids to the carnival and showed the parents where the food line began. We started raffling off gift cards and giving away coupons for free turkeys for Thanksgiving, which was right around the corner. I watched as families from our suburban church sat down and dined and laughed with families of South Central. It was amazing.

As the barbecue wound down and our team began to clean up, I noticed a few teenage girls bickering. I love young people in middle school and high school. I just get them. So I approached the girls and quickly identified the ringleader.

"Hi, girls."

No one said anything, so I said it again, this time looking the ringleader directly in the face. "Hello."

She looked at me and said, "So?"

"So, what's your name?"

"Why?" she retorted.

"Because usually when you meet someone, you say, 'Hi. I'm Shelene. What's your name?'"

"Jessie," she replied.

"Oh, hey, Jessie. What's the matter? You look a bit upset."

"Yeah, I am. I didn't get a gift card." She glared at the girl on her right, who had a gift card in her hand.

"Oh, really?" I said. "Well, what gift card did you want?"

"One of those Target gift cards."

"We are out, but I'll tell you what. Why don't you give me your phone number, and after Christmas I'll come and pick you up and take you shopping at Target?"

"Yeah, right. I'm never going to see you again after today."

"Well then, why not give me your number and take a chance?"

"Do it," the girl on Jessie's right whispered while elbowing her. "Do it."

"Yeah, Jessie. Do it. You have nothing to lose," I said as I handed her a pen.

Jessie grabbed my hand and wrote her phone number on my palm. Gotta love it.

"Nice meeting you, Jessie. I'll see you soon."

"Bye," the other two girls said, giggling.

"Bye," Jessie said under her breath.

As our team piled into my car, Jessie was the talk of the night. Believe me when I tell you everyone was rocked that day. Our whole team met and heard stories that were inspiring but also heartbreaking.

But I was not expecting what happened to me that night. I fell in *love* with that girl. I couldn't get her off my heart. And I thought about her and wondered if the number she wrote on my hand was even real.

Lord, forgive me for being fearful and for allowing that fear to dictate my actions. Give me the faith to be willing to follow Your call, even when it makes me uncomfortable. Help me never forget that You are in complete control of all things. Give me the wisdom not to neglect Your best for me because I am chained by fear. May I be strong and courageous and not be terrified, for You are with me wherever I go. Most of all, help me have open eyes to the physical and spiritual needs of those I come into contact with. Amen.

TEN

Call Me, Maybe?

On January 2, I made the call. As I began to dial the numbers the teenaged Jessie had written on my hand two months earlier, I expected to hear the familiar *doo-doo-doo* tones and the announcement, "We're sorry; you have reached a number that has been disconnected or is no longer in service. If you feel you have reached this recording in error, please check the number and try your call again."

To my surprise, the phone started to ring. Then it kept ringing. It rang and rang, and just before I was about to hang up, I heard a sharp, irritated voice yell into the phone, *"Hello!"*

"Oh, hi," I said as pleasantly as I could. "Is Jessie there?"

"Why?" the voice on the other end demanded.

"Why? Uh, well, because I'm Shelene, and I met her at the—"

Before I could get the words out of my mouth, the voice on the other end of the phone yelled, *"Mom*, it's that white girl from the barbecue."

"Oh, hi, Jessie. That must be you."

"Hi, Shelene," she said, with what sounded like a smile in her voice.

"Well, are you ready to go shopping?"

"*Yes!*"

Now I knew for sure she was smiling. We made arrangements for me to pick her up on Saturday.

When Saturday morning arrived, I headed out to spend the day with my young new friend. As I exited the freeway, I was sure not to miss my turn this time.

I pulled up to an old, unkempt apartment building that brought new meaning to the word *slumlord*. The two-story structure was so weathered and broken down I was afraid to sneeze for fear it might come crashing down.

Of course Jessie's apartment was on the top floor. The open-air staircase seemed to be right out of a Tim Burton cartoon: the spaces between each stair slat were so big I was certain every other step was missing.

As I walked by each apartment on my way to hers, I noticed many apartment doors were wide open. I could not help but peek in. Most apartments had a single mattress lying flat on the living room floor. Little babies seemed to be everywhere. Two or three women appeared in some of the doors. I smiled, but no one cared.

Before I could reach Jessie's door, she ran out.

"You're here! You came."

"Yes, of course I did."

As I turned around and started to walk down the stairs, two more girls came running out and followed us down to my car. I unlocked the doors, and all three girls jumped in.

The girls looked vaguely familiar to me, and they reminded me that they were the ones with Jessie at the barbecue. Lora was the one who'd been lambasted by my precious Jessie because she had won a gift card and Jessie had not. Lisa was Lora's sister.

"Well, are you all ready?"

"Yes!" they chimed in unison.

"Great. So, where are your mothers? I'd like to meet them and make sure they are okay with this complete stranger taking you in her SUV to a mall that's most likely twenty miles from here."

Lisa quickly answered, "Well, our mom's at work, and I'm in charge, so it's okay for us to go with you."

"Oh, okay," I said. "And you, Jessie?"

In response, she rolled her window down, leaned her thin body out the passenger side window, looked up, and yelled, *"Mom!"*

Remarkably, I heard, *"What?"* coming from the second-story penthouse.

"Come out here," Jessie shouted.

The apartment door swung open, and a lady with a child on her hip stepped out onto the rickety terrace.

I jumped out of my car and said, "Hi. I'm Shelene. I met your daughter at the barbecue—"

She quickly interrupted me and said, "I know who you are."

"Well, then may I please take your daughter—"

Again cutting me off mid-sentence, *"Yes,* take her. Take her, please."

"Great. What time would you like me to have her back?"

"Whenever is fine."

With that, we were off to find the closest, safest mall around without having to go to Beverly Hills.

As we reached the mall, I told the girls that I would like to buy them each a new outfit. They smiled and excitedly piled out of the car and we made our way into Macy's.

I told the girls to pick tons of options to try on. As I turned, I saw all three girls grabbing underwear and socks.

I blurted out, "What are you doing?"

"Getting underwear and socks," Jessie said.

"I see that, but I want to get you girls something that everyone can see, a cute outfit, jeans, jackets, boots, dresses, whatever you want."

"Can we still get the underwear and socks?" one of them asked.

"Yes, of course," and with that the shopping spree began.

When at last the young salesgirl rang up our order and took off the security sensors, I sent the girls into the dressing room to put on their new clothes.

It is important to note here that money to buy new outfits does not change lives. In fact, some of the most powerful life-changing times I have seen have been when resources have been scarce. God is the heart changer and life changer, and money is rarely the way by which He effects real change. We have to recognize that even when money is tight, we can still help people in need.

God knows you and knows everything about your circumstances, and He will put the people in your path He wants you to impact. God did not need my money to take care of Jessie; He is always the provider. He wanted my heart to show love to a young girl who needed Him.

As we loaded back into the car, I asked them, "If you could go anywhere for dinner, where would you like to go?"

"Anywhere?"

"Yes, anywhere," I answered.

Whispers and snickers came from the backseat.

"Well, where will it be? Your chauffeur awaits."

"I don't know," Jessie said.

"Yes you do."

In the back of my mind I wondered, *Are they going to say Ivy at the Shore or Spago or something outrageous?*

"Okay," Jessie said. "If we can really go anywhere . . . can we go to Sizzler?"

"Sizzler?"

"Yes! Sizzler," they all said in unison, with huge smiles on their faces.

"Okay, Sizzler it is."

Now, if I only knew where the heck a Sizzler was around here.

I hadn't been to a Sizzler in years but remembered always liking it. As we walked up to order, I had forgotten that the menu was written on a huge board on the front wall of the restaurant.

I told the girls to get whatever they'd like.

Lora and Lisa quickly placed their orders.

Then it was Jessie's turn.

"A lot of choices, huh?"

"Yeah," she said, looking up at the board.

As the seconds ticked on into minutes, the line behind us started to get impatient.

"Well, what do you want, Jessie?"

"I don't know," she said.

"What do you mean you don't know? You picked this place. Get whatever you want; it's on me."

"You order for me," she said as she continued to stare blankly at the menu board. Just then it hit me.

"Jessie, can you read that board, honey?"

Dropping her head, she whispered in shame, "No, I can't."

"Okay, then let me tell you what your choices are."

We ordered and joined the other two girls at the table.

At this point I was dying inside. How was it that this thirteen-year-old girl in the Los Angeles Unified School System was just getting passed along and couldn't even read a Sizzler menu?

During dinner I found out Jessie had a twin brother, Josh, and their dad was in San Quentin State Prison. Little did the girls know they were going to be seeing a lot more of Aunt Shelene.

My next lunch would be with their moms. Oh, how God loves to take us out of our comfort zones and bring us face-to-face with Him. I had no idea that just 38.7 miles from my house was this community and these families that I was going to fall in love with.

In the days, weeks, months, and years that followed the community barbecue, God allowed a sweet season to pass in my life. I got to meet with Jessie's teachers about getting her extra help with reading; we had a friend donate a car to Jessie's family; another friend donated furniture for the girls' apartments. Their moms received a scholarship to join me at a women's retreat in the mountains at beautiful Lake Arrowhead and got to hear about God's acceptance, love, and forgiveness. The residual fingerprints of those moments with those families can still be seen in my life today.

I believe the reason my experience in South Central Los

Angeles had such an inspirational impact on my life was because my whole experience involved the concept of *jump*. I was willing to jump in and be extremely uncomfortable.

As I wrote in chapter 4, jumping is really just the act of saying yes to God and taking an action, a choice followed by movement, a decision resulting in moving feet. Richard and Shelly Brown are a perfect example of extreme jumpers. Richard went all in, in response to how God was tugging on his heart. Shelly's candid honesty revealed that if she had followed her initial feelings and refrained from going to South Central, she would have missed out on an amazing adventure God had planned for her life.

I used to think that I had to feel great about what God wanted me to do. I have learned, though, that you don't always immediately feel good about obeying God. I was feeling out of my comfort zone just to be involved in a neighborhood that looked vastly different from mine. How many times have I let my feelings get in the way of an incredible journey that God wanted to take me on?

The fact is, our feelings are extremely deceptive and do not necessarily have a relationship to truth. Often when we act in obedience to God, the positive feelings will come later.

Jumping involves putting our feelings of fear, hurt, or anger aside, taking a step of faith, and doing what God has asked us to do. Jumping involves a pure yes to God, an undefiled, unselfish yes, not expecting anything in return.

So often when we finally jump, our *"yes!"* to God leads us and others around us to experience His true love. You can experience the incredible joyfulness God gives those who actually are doers of His Word, not just hearers.

Lord, help me look beyond economic and cultural divides to see the faces of the people You want me to love. Give me the courage to boldly go to places to break down with Your love and kindness the barriers our society has thrown up. Provide me the strength to jump into the tasks and relationships You want to use to draw me closer to You. Let me experience the joy of not only hearing Your Word but doing it. Amen.

ELEVEN

Secret Agent Girl

Five days after I turned twenty-one, I was approached by a family friend, Brad, who was a special agent for the Department of Justice. They were looking for just the right person to pull off an undercover sting that involved setting up "call girl" operations with the ability to accept credit card payments for their services. Specifically, Justice needed someone who could sell credit card processing services and convince the madams they needed this service and that it was completely trustworthy. Basically, the government needed a fast-talking salesperson who could overcome any objection and set up career criminals with this credit card service that would later be used to bust their prostitution ring. That's where I came in.

Brad had known me since I was a young girl and over the years had watched me talk just about anyone into anything. As a child I had managed to talk the clerks at the local 7-Eleven into giving me free Slurpees and Milky Way bars by telling them I'd bring a bunch of kids from my school to their store. Brad always said, "Shelene, you could sell snow to a snowman." He knew I was just the person who could make this sting operation happen and be a success. Brad arranged a meeting with the special agent in charge of the sting.

As the day of the meeting approached, my excitement began to build. This was really cool. I was going to be an undercover secret agent girl. Of course I watched every spy movie I could get my hands on leading up to my meeting. I went to the mall and bought a dark blue wool suit. Every movie I saw with a female special agent had very cool, rather short, dark blue skirt-and-blazer suits. I had to look the part.

When the meeting day finally arrived, Brad and I drove to Marie Callender's on Ventura Boulevard in Studio City, California. We were ushered to a booth and waited for Mr. 007 to arrive.

When I caught my first glimpse of the agent, I was not disappointed—he was right out of my movie imagination. He was in his early thirties, a little over six feet tall, fit, with short sandy-blond hair, brown eyes, and a warm smile.

I stood to introduce myself.

"Hi, I'm Shelene," I said as I extended my hand.

"Hi," he said with a kind smile and a firm handshake. "I know who you are."

"Oh, great. Yeah, I guess you would." I chuckled.

We sat down and he got right to business.

"Brad speaks very highly of you. He says you're just the girl to pull off the operation he told you about."

"Yes, I am."

"Let me explain what we need you to do, and then you can tell me if you still want to be involved."

He proceeded to explain how I would be making cold telephone calls to various escort services while tape-recording the conversations for evidence.

"Also, if you want to give this a shot, I will train you on the devices and phone taps we need you to use."

I sat listening quietly, suddenly feeling the weight of this undertaking.

"We will need you to have a phone tap in place on every call you make. Never call a potential suspect without logging and recording each call. Understand?"

"Yes," I said much more confidently than I felt.

"Good," he said. "Now, a lot of these call girl rings operate out of nightclubs. What you'll do is call the establishment, ask for the general manager or whoever handles and makes decisions regarding MasterCard and Visa devices. Tell them that you can beat any transaction fee they're currently paying. You can save them thousands of dollars in processing fees. Your whole goal will be to set up a face-to-face meeting with the club owner, manager, or madam. The moment you have one set up, let me know."

Sweet, I was thinking. *I am going to impress the heck out of this guy, and before you know it, they will want me full-time at the FBI.*

After I told him that I was in, he had me sign some paperwork and provided me with a box filled with all my secret agent stuff. He patiently walked through every item: the phone tap, which had a round hoop microphone that attached to any landline handset; the tape recorder; the portable MasterCard/Visa machine that was the size of a man's wallet. The small credit card machine came with a special plastic spoon that the girls could use to slide credit cards and make the much-needed impression.

Three very large yellow pages phone books were provided with various escort services highlighted. Yes, these services actually had the guts to advertise in the yellow pages. Of course the ads contained only "deniable" content.

Mr. 007 told me most credit card companies offer 2.5 to

3 percent on all credit card transaction fees. "You, Shelene, can charge whatever you want. We have been authorized to go as low as half a percent."

"Easy," I said. "I'm never going that low. The first thing I learned in Sales 101 is if it seems too good to be true, it probably is. Believe me, these people graduated from the school of hard knocks. They will sniff out 'too good to be true' in a heartbeat. I need to stay competitive but maybe start them with a low fee to hook them in, then tell them it will bump up to 2 percent after the first year, still saving them tons of money."

Mr. 007 threw Brad an amused glance and smile. "She's good. I like this girl." Then to me he said, "You are going to be perfect."

"Great," I said. "When can I start?"

"Give me a day to process the paperwork. I'll call you tomorrow, and you should be able to start tomorrow night." Then he handed me his card. "Please call me right away, day or night, if you book an appointment. I need to know ASAP."

I wanted to say, "You mean *when* I book an appointment," but "Will do" is what came out of my mouth. Nice to meet you, Mr. Good-Looking Secret Agent Man.

Driving home from the meeting, down the 101 Ventura freeway, I was on top of the world. The top was down, and as the wind was blowing at my hair, I imagined me and hunky Mr. 007 handcuffing the bad guys (or girls, as it were).

When I got home, I had to make several trips to and from the driveway to unload all the equipment I had just been issued. As I set up the equipment on the family phone and began to try it out by calling my friends, all of a sudden I was gripped by a panic. *What are you doing, Shelene? You are about to make these calls out of your bedroom? Are you crazy?* My mind began to race.

I thought to myself, *If I have all this high-tech stuff, then the bad guys will probably have equipment so they can trace me. Once they trace me, they might come and kidnap my sister and kill my family.*

I think I watched too many *Godfather* and other mobster movies. So to avoid the carnage and havoc on my unsuspecting family, I decided to make my calls from outside my house, from a location that would scare even the most hardened criminal: the church. My future husband, Brice (then a sincere dating interest), was the youth pastor at Simi Community Church. He said I could use his office to do my calling. If anyone tracked me, it would lead the bad guy to the church. I figured that's where they needed to be anyway. Perfect idea, Brice.

I got one of the highlighted phone books and started calling nightclubs in the Los Angeles area.

"Studio 10," the gruff, I-smoke-three-packs-a-day-sounding female voice on the other end of the line said.

"Hi. This is Kim," I said, using the alias Mr. 007 and I had agreed on. "Can I speak to whoever's in charge?"

"Well, okay, honey. Dancer auditions are on Tuesdays. Call back tomorrow afternoon at three and ask for Cindy."

"Wait," I said before she could hang up the phone. "I'm not a dancer, but what I have will make your boss super happy."

"Well, I'm the boss, so, honey, whatcha sellin'?"

I bolted upright in my chair. I had made twenty calls, and the extent of my progress had been several answering machines and even more low-level idiots who sounded like real winners. But now I had a real madam actually on the phone.

My heart was racing, but as calmly as I could, I replied, "Well, not really selling anything. I mean, it wouldn't cost you a dime. Do your girls take credit cards?"

"Yeah. So what?"

"Well, what's your rate?"

A few minutes into my pitch, I could tell I was starting to make some headway.

"So you're telling me I could reduce my rate from five to one and a half percent?" the woman snapped.

"Well, that's just an introductory rate for the first six months. Then it bumps to 2 percent, which sounds like a substantial savings over your current rate."

"Sweetheart, I run all my bills through a flower shop. Can you set that up for me like my other processer?" she wheezed.

"Absolutely not a problem. I can run it through a flower shop, a gym, or even a doughnut shop if you need me to!" I had no idea if that was true or even doable, but I figured Mr. 007 had the resources of the entire government behind him, so it should be no problem.

A few minutes later I had secured a meeting with the madam. I hung up the phone and jumped around the office in celebration.

After my first night on the phone, I had set up three appointments using my fake name, Kim. It was about one thirty in the morning when I finished. Remembering that Mr. 007 had said to call him ASAP, that's exactly what I did. There must be something about the training these special agents do, because when he answered the phone, it was as if he'd been waiting for my call. I had been afraid I was going to wake him, but he sounded like he had been up for hours.

"Hi. It's me, Shelene."

"Yes, I know," he said.

"Oh, of course you do. Great. Well, I have set up three appointments for us for next week."

"Three! Wow. Great work, Shelene."

"Thank you," I said, with a huge smile. Thank goodness he couldn't see me through the phone with that stupid grin plastered all over my face. "I set them up at the location you requested, but one guy asked if we could meet him at his club for lunch. I told him no problem. Was that okay?"

"Yes," he said.

Feeling a bit like a rock star, I said, "So where do you want to meet before the meetings?"

"You're not," Mr. 007 answered.

"What?" I blurted out.

"Shelene, you can't go to these meetings—"

Before he could finish his sentence, I cut him off. "But they are expecting to meet Kim, a woman—me."

"I understand," he said. "That's why I'll be bringing my partner, a woman, with me."

"But they don't know her. They know me and my voice."

"Shelene, you're not a trained law enforcement agent. I would never want to put you or me in danger. Unfortunately it's just not possible."

"Right," I said, embarrassed and thinking to myself, *I'm a fake agent. The real agent, the trained agent, the qualified agent, will go to the meeting.* "Copy that."

He must have felt the wind come out of my wings because he said kindly, "Shelene, what you did tonight was huge. We have been calling to get into these clubs for weeks without a single appointment. You hooked us up with three stings in one night. That is phenomenal. Please keep up the good work."

"Okay," I said, feeling a small smile brush across my face. "I will."

This experience helped me realize the value in being the real thing. You see, for much of my young adult life, I was faking something far more important than being a secret agent. I was faking being a Christian. It was not even an intentional deception. I had learned all the Christian lingo, I could quote verses, and I could even suck people into a good story about Jesus. But I was missing what it meant to surrender the controls of my life over to God.

Many people are faking the Christian life without even knowing it. They can show up at church and talk the talk but don't have a true relationship with God. They don't know what it means to follow hard after Christ. Some of us are missing heaven by eighteen inches—the distance between our heads and our hearts. We have all the knowledge in our heads. We know the right things to say or do, but we don't really follow God with our hearts, our everything. God draws the line at my heart.

I was a fake special agent. I could learn the lingo, have all the special gadgets, but I had no training, experience, and most of all, no commitment to be a real, bona fide agent.

I grew up going to church on Sundays, and I was taught to be a good girl, which I was. A good girl was someone who didn't smoke, drink, take drugs, or sleep with her boyfriend. Everything else was fair game.

I was so busy trying to measure my goodness against my friends' that most of the time I looked really good. By all accounts I was a good Christian girl. I had learned "churchese." I could recite all the books of the Bible in order and would win Bible verse look-up drills. I was so wrapped up in the behaviorism the church had taught me, I thought I was for sure going to heaven.

For some reason I had it in my head that God graded on a curve. If God lined up all humanity on Judgment Day in order from good to bad, with Mother Teresa on one end and Osama bin Laden on the other, I wouldn't look too bad. Compared to the people on the bad end, I'm really good. I was certainly on the high end of the bell curve.

The problem is, God does not grade on a curve. I was completely missing it.

The amazing thing is, if you are reading this right now and are not sure if you have been faking it, you still have a chance to change that today. *Now!*

Tomorrow is promised to no one. There is absolutely no guarantee you will wake up in the morning. My question to you is, are you really prepared for what happens after you die? My fear is that some of you will answer, "Yes, I'm prepared" too quickly and skip this chapter and someday find that you had deceived yourself without appropriately considering this passage:

[Jesus] told them this parable: "The ground of a certain rich man yielded an abundant harvest. He thought to himself, 'What shall I do? I have no place to store my crops.'

"Then he said, 'This is what I'll do. I will tear down

my barns and build bigger ones, and there I will store my surplus grain. And I'll say to myself, "You have plenty of grain laid up for many years. Take life easy; eat, drink and be merry."'

"But God said to him, 'You fool! This very night your life will be demanded from you. Then who will get what you have prepared for yourself?'

"This is how it will be with whoever stores up things for themselves but is not rich toward God." (Luke 12:16–21)

It is very easy to forget that we will someday be face-to-face with the living God. There is a 100 percent mortality rate. Everyone reading this book will die. Each one of us has an expiration date only known to God. It could be forty years from now; it could be tomorrow.

Have you ever considered the Ten Commandments? In a recent survey, eight out of ten Americans said they "believed" in the Ten Commandments. But many people don't understand they are the laws of God, His standard of behavior for humans. The problem is, we cannot keep the commandments.

Even though I had grown up going to church my whole life, when a friend asked me to name the Ten Commandments, I failed miserably. I began to realize that even though I had listened to sermons on them, talked about them, and thought I knew them, I had never really actually read them (they're in Exodus 20).

After reviewing the Ten Commandments, I thought, *That is really depressing. Who can ever get to heaven?* If God demands perfection, we are all doomed. We have all lied. We have all stolen something (including things of small value, like someone else's answers when we cheated on a test, or a grape in the market that we wanted to "test"). Well, the truth is, it would be depressing if the story ended there. But it doesn't.

Here is the best news of your life: *Despite everything you and I have done in our lives, God loves you and me and does not want to punish us.*

In the greatest act of love of all time, God Himself had His Son come down to earth in the form of a man, Jesus. God's plan was that Jesus would be nailed to a cross and die as punishment for *our* sins.

After thinking on the Ten Commandments, I realized I was guilty. I was not the good person I thought I was. I had lied. I had stolen things. I had taken the Lord's name in vain. The Bible says the punishment for any of that is death: "The wages of sin is death" (Romans 6:23).

Understand something—I am not arrogantly a Christian. I suck and need a Savior. That is why Jesus' sacrifice on the cross means so much to me. I hope you will take the time to read the Ten Commandments in Exodus and ask yourself this question: Am I innocent, or guilty of breaking His laws? If you came up with the same answer I did, there is still an opportunity to turn and run toward the cross. We are saved by the undeserved favor of God alone, so that no man or woman may boast.

If this is the only chapter of this whole book that you read, if this is the only *yes* you say in your entire life, don't miss it. You might need to go get alone with God in prayer and acknowledge you have messed up, admit you have faults. Ask for forgiveness. Tell God that you want to be in a relationship with Him. Then you need to follow God.

That's what makes Christ's blood on the cross so powerful.

Please don't ever think there is a mistake you have made that is too great for the blood of Christ to handle. God is a God of second chances.

"Why, you do not even know what will happen tomorrow," the apostle James wrote. "What is your life? You are a mist that appears for a little while and then vanishes" (James 4:14).

Jesus taught that wide is the road that leads to destruction, but narrow is the road that leads to everlasting life, and few find it. Which road are you on? My wish for you is that you become one of the few who find the narrow road. Don't miss Him.

Lord, my faults have alienated me from You. For reasons I do not compre-hend, despite everything I have done, You still love me and do not want to punish me. In Your great, unexplainable mercy, You gave Your only Son to pay the penalty for my failures. Thank You for that sacrifice for me. I am so grateful for that undeserved act of love. Help me live a life that is worthy of that love. Amen.

TWELVE

Landlord from Heaven

I was in the market for professional office space for my expanding talent promotion business. After much review I found a really cool office building in Calabasas. Calabasas is the westernmost city in the San Fernando Valley of Los Angeles County, the home to many of the studios in Los Angeles: Disney, Warner Brothers, and Universal, just to name a few.

I spotted a clean, modern architecture building with a Southern California Spanish look. The underground parking sold me. *This must be crazy expensive*, I thought. I called the owner's leasing agent, who said his name was Jeff, and I set a time to meet him at suite 108.

When I walked into the suite, I instantly fell in love with the space. I got that this-is-the-place feeling. "I love it," I said. "How much?"

"Well," Jeff said, "let's go to my office and see what we can do."

Knowing it was time to start talking money, I explained to Jeff that I had none. My business was a startup. I was borrowing every dime to get started.

After sympathetically listening to my sob story, he said, "Here's what I can do: I can temporarily give the space to you month to month for a buck a square foot, but I will continue to show it, and if someone is willing to pay the going rate, you match it or you're out. After one year, the rent goes up to the going rate, which is double what I just quoted you."

"Great. That sounds super fair," I said. "Let me talk to my husband and I'll be in touch."

When Brice looked at the space, he loved it. He was a bit suspicious about the low price, but he said, "If the price he gave you is true, let's do it. I am absolutely in."

I called Jeff and told him we had a deal and set up a meeting time to sign the lease.

The next afternoon Brice and I arrived at the Calabasas building, where Jeff's office was. As we walked in, the grand glass and black marble spiraling staircase was a bit intimidating. With my high heels on, it felt as if anyone within a ten-mile radius could hear me clomping up those stairs. As we reached the top, we saw a beautiful, all-glass conference room on our left, and a sweet little old receptionist greeted us from the right side of the reception landing.

"Hi," I said. "We're here for Jeff, to sign a lease."

"Sure," she said. "Have a seat. He will be right with you."

As soon as we sat down, we heard a deep, resonating sound clacking its way up the spiral staircase, accompanied by what sounded like panting. This sound made my earlier, three-inch-heel clomping seem quite mild. Brice gave me a funny look, as if to say, *What the heck is that?* and got up to see what was making all the racket. As he turned around toward the stairs, a massive, black-and-white, lovable Old English sheepdog appeared at the top of the stairs.

The dog went straight to Brice, and Brice went straight for

the dog. Brice knelt down on one knee and gave that fluffy dog a big hug and rubdown. Just as the two of them were getting acquainted, a classy, pretty, fit, early-fortyish-looking lady reached the top of the stairs.

"Nikki!" she called.

Immediately the dog (apparently, Nikki) left Brice and heeled at his owner's side.

"So sorry about that. He has not seen me in a couple of weeks and got a bit excited."

"Oh, no problem," Brice said. "I love your dog. When I was a kid, I worked at a pet store and saved all summer for a dog that looked just like him."

"Really," the sweet lady said warmly. "I'm Kay," extending a hand. "Nice to meet you. We just got back from a trip to Aspen, and I came to pick him up."

Kay smiled at the receptionist and then escorted Nikki down the stairs.

Just then Jeff appeared. "Hi, guys," he said. "Let's go into the conference room and sign the lease and then get you the keys to your new office."

"Great," I said. At that moment I had no idea the impact leasing this office suite was going to have on our lives, our future family's life, and ultimately, my walk with God.

———

I spent the next few weeks getting settled into my new office space. I spent the next several months consumed with building my talent management business. Brice kept on working full time and attending law school full time in the evenings. I have to admit, the year flew by.

Before I knew it, Jeff was back in my office, letting me know my options.

"How's business?" he asked.

"Great," I said.

"Good. So you'd like to stay in this suite?"

"Stay in this suite? I just got here. I'm just getting started."

"Well," Jeff said, "I want to remind you about your lease. We put you in this space at a really cheap rate, and now that you're on your feet, it's time you pay the going rate."

"Oh yeah . . . right," I said. "What is the going rate?"

"I hate to say it, but your rent is going to double."

"What? I can't afford that. Oh my. Is there anything you can do?"

"No," Jeff said. "That was the deal."

"Okay. Let me talk to my husband."

My poor husband. Just as the ink was beginning to dry on my classy business cards and my company was starting to thrive, it looked as though I was going to need to shut it down.

That night I explained the situation to Brice. "Let's pray right now," he said.

After we prayed, Brice said, "I think you should see if you can get a meeting with the owner of the building and just be honest. Explain to him your situation."

"Okay," I agreed.

The next morning I put a call in to Jeff and asked if he could please set up a meeting with the owner of the building.

"We usually can't do that, but I'll see what I can do."

The next day Jeff informed me that the owner, Mr. Dickens,

could meet with me the following morning at nine. That night I stayed late at the office, packing up a few things, realizing that the odds of staying in this amazing building for another month were slim to none. Although I was new to the building, all I ever heard from my fellow tenants was that the owner was a multimillionaire who did not like his tenants very much.

The morning meeting came quickly enough. There I was, back in my landlord's intimidating office suite, with the spiraling marble staircase and the fish bowl of a conference room. As I clinked my way back up those stairs for a second time, I thought, *Really? Did I really just wear high heels again?* I wanted to kick myself.

The now-familiar receptionist greeted me. As she escorted me into the conference room, I could feel and hear my heart trying to beat right out of my chest.

Suddenly a thin, distinguished, six-foot-three businessman walked in. I jumped up to introduce myself.

"Hi, I'm Shelene Bryan. You must be Mr. Dickens."

"Yes, I am," he said in a sharp tone.

"Great. Well, I'm in suite 108, and I have a proposal I'd like to present to you. I was extremely fortunate to get into this building almost a year ago for a dollar a square foot. My problem is, things are just now starting to take off. If my rent goes up to where you want it to go, I will be driven out of business." My mouth was clearly in overdrive running a mile a minute. *Slow down, Shelene.*

I took out a sheet of paper containing my proposal of gradual increases of rent and spread it on the conference table.

Dead silence fell over the room. Then he spoke. "Why should you pay any less than anyone else in my building?"

"I guess I shouldn't," I replied, "but I do pay my rent on time every month, and from what I can see, I'm one of your youngest tenants, which means I'm more likely to be around a bit longer than the older folks I see all over the building. Besides, I just love it here and really don't want to have to move next month."

Silence again fell over the room.

Finally, he said, "Well, leave me your proposal and I'll look it over. Now you get down there and make some money."

Was that a hint of a smile on his lips?

"Okay, thank you. Thank you very much, sir," I said as I backed my way out of the conference room door.

I flew down the spiral staircase, my *clack*s echoing all the way. Then I hightailed it back to my office. I couldn't get to my phone fast enough to call Brice.

"Hi. How did it go?" he asked.

"Not well. We should probably start packing up my office. At the end of the month, I'm going to be booted out of here."

I didn't sleep a wink that night. The conversation with Mr. Dickens ran over and over again in my mind.

When I arrived the next day at my office, Jeff, the property manager, greeted me. "What did you say to Mr. Dickens?" he asked, agitation in his voice.

"I just showed him my idea about the gradual rent bumpups. He didn't seem too thrilled. He told me to get back down to my office and make some money."

"Well," Jeff said, "I've worked for this man for years, and I've never seen him react this way before."

"React what way?"

"This morning I asked if he wanted me to start showing your suite. He said, 'No, just leave her alone. She can stay for what she's paying now.'"

"What?" I said in disbelief.

"Yep. He said you can just stay in 108 month to month at a buck a square foot. Just don't be late on the rent. Frankly, I can't believe it."

"Oh my goodness! Thank you, Jeff. Thank you very much."

I was working late the next day and remembered seeing Mr. Dickens's light on in his suite late some nights too. That gave me an idea. I decided to go home at lunch and work up a thank-you dinner for him and write him a thank-you card. I went to Costco and got a frozen lasagna, opened the package, poured some Ragu on the top, and added some grated cheese. I also bought a fresh loaf of French bread.

That night, true to form, it looked like Mr. Dickens's office light was burning.

As I got to the top of the grand winding staircase, I noticed all the lights were off but one.

"Hello? Helloo?"

No answer. I decided to walk to the back, where I saw the office light on.

The door was cracked a little, and I pushed it open with my foot while balancing the lasagna and bread.

As I entered the office, I saw a man sitting behind a desk. Startled, he looked up. It was Mr. Dickens. He looked as if he'd been crying.

I put down the lasagna and French bread. "Are you okay?" I asked.

"No, not really," he said.

"Well, I made you some dinner to warm up. I wanted to thank you for your kindness. I won't let you down."

"Okay," he said. "Thank you."

Without being invited, I sat down in one of the chairs across from his big, beautiful desk. I reached my hands out across his desk, palms up, and asked, "Can I pray for you?"

"You don't even know what you're praying about," he said.

"That's okay—God does."

He reached his hands out and placed them in mine.

"Dear God, I don't know what Mr. Dickens is going through tonight, but I know You do. You absolutely know every little detail of his troubles. I pray You will give him the strength to face whatever battle he needs to face."

When I finished praying, he thanked me and said, "It's my wife. She's a really healthy woman. She's only fifty. She eats good, runs two miles almost every day. Two weeks ago we went out to dinner. When we got back to the house, she asked me to get her a wet washcloth because she wasn't feeling well. I went to the sink and before I knew it, she had blacked out." His voice cracked with emotion.

Kay . . . the pretty lady with the sheepdog, I thought.

"I dialed 911," he went on. "By the time the paramedics arrived, she was awake and coherent. They asked if she still wanted to go to the hospital. Kay said yes, she thought she should. I followed the ambulance to the hospital."

After arriving at the hospital, he told me, a doctor walked up to him and said, "Your wife has an aneurism on her brain. We need to go in and do emergency surgery and put a plate over it to contain it, or she will die." He told the doctor he would like to get a second opinion from UCLA or Cedars.

"Kay and I don't have any kids, so I had to make all these decisions alone and very fast," he said.

The doctor had told him, "If you take your wife, you will need to sign her out AMA [against medical advice]. Your wife's aneurism is like a grenade, and the pin has been pulled. If you move her, you take the risk of killing her."

"What did you do?" I asked him.

"What could I do? I agreed to have the doctor do the surgery. I didn't want to lose my wife."

"What happened after the surgery?"

"Well, the doctor went in to treat the aneurism, and the brain surgery caused Kay to have two back-to-back strokes. She is completely paralyzed. Her hands went back to the fetal position. She can't walk or talk, she has a G-tube in to feed her, and to be honest, I don't know the extent of the brain damage."

"Can I go see her?" I asked.

"Sure," he said. "I was on my way there before you walked in."

"Great. My husband is in law school and doesn't get home until ten thirty. Why don't we go check on Kay and then have dinner?"

———

It was that one *yes* moment that started a beautiful relationship. Within a year Mr. Dickens's hard exterior melted away. He had become "Pops." And Kay made a turn for the better. Although she had suffered massive brain damage and was still paralyzed, Pops was eventually able to bring her home to full-time nursing care.

Our kids have called them Grampie Al and Grandma Kay since they were born. Pops and Kay spend every Christmas, Easter, and birthday with us.

Someone once told Jesus, "Your mother and brothers are standing outside, wanting to speak to you."

"Who is my mother and who are my brothers?" He asked. Then, pointing to His disciples, He answered, "Here are my mother and my brothers, for whoever does the will of my Father in heaven is my brother and sister and mother" (Matthew 12:47–50, paraphrased).

As Christians, anyone who does the will of our Father in heaven is our family.

The relationship with Pops and Kay would begin to teach me about the family of God, the way God intended it to be. Pops would eventually teach me about money, and I was on a mission to teach him about Jesus. Kay had loved the Lord before she got sick and would pray for her husband every day. Pops, on the other hand, believed in being a man of his word, making as much money as possible, and not a whole lot else.

We began to have dinner with Pops and Kay every week. What an amazing joy it was for me to at last see Pops accept Christ as his Lord and Savior.

As Pops and I continued to meet every week, God started softening his heart. We had been studying about serving God with our gifts. Gifts from God are not gifts for us to keep and hoard, but are for us to steward. Pops was not one to stand up in front of a crowd and teach a Bible study, but when it came to building a commercial building, no one was better.

One week Pops said, "Shelene, I think the Lord is calling me to build the new church building at Cornerstone."

"What? Really?" I said.

"Yes, honey. Can you please set up a meeting with whomever I need to meet with about that?"

"Of course. I would love to."

The joy in his voice still rings in my ears today. God doesn't want us to do anything without joy. When it comes to serving God with our gifts, it's not a "have to," it's a "get to." We *get* to say yes and change everything. Pops was about to start his second *yes* ripple. The first was when, by faith, he said yes and gave his life over to the Lord. Now he was saying yes to something that a few months earlier would have seemed like foolishness.

Brice made the call to our pastor and set up a meeting.

Pops, as an architect and builder, was disappointed to find out that a different architect had already drawn up plans, and that if he wanted to build the church, he would need to build according to the plans already approved. He made it clear that he was not happy with the artistic design of the project, and it was killing him to build a structure that was not to his taste. I told him that God likes to teach us humility right away in our walk with Him.

He said, "Honey, I really feel God wants me to do this, even with the existing plans."

The elder board and pastors were elated. They had received several bids from contractors to build the church, but once Pops, who hates to waste money, looked over everything, he told the church that he would build the church for cost, that he wasn't looking to make any money off the church. He just wanted to do what he felt God was asking of him.

The project ended up saving the church hundreds of thousands of dollars. The next closest bidder was called in and told he was not doing the job. That contractor called Pops the next day and asked to keep his signs up around the project. "Everyone thinks I'm building this church," he said, "so if I could keep them up, it would sure be great."

"Sure," Pops said. "I don't care who knows I'm building it. I'm a new Christian and just trying to do what God asked."

Without even knowing the Bible verse that says, "Don't let your right hand know what your left hand is doing" or the one that says, "You can either get your applause from man or wait and get it from Me in heaven,"[1] Pops was being the church.

Pops and Kay are still going strong, and Pops is home every night by six to see his sweet bride, who can really do nothing material for him. Her speech is limited; she can't walk, can't eat, and can't care for him in the way a husband needs. Her favorite things are Jesus, going to the movies, and never missing church on Sundays. God has a special place in heaven for Kay where she won't need her wheelchair anymore—where Kay and Pops can talk, walk, run, swim, eat, and laugh.

Pops chose his wife before God to love, cherish, honor, and adore, in sickness and in health, till death do they part. With his resources he could have put Kay in a posh Beverly Hills care facility and found a girlfriend. Most people wouldn't have blamed him, and some think he's a fool for not doing it and enjoying the rest of his life with a healthy woman. Instead, Pops said *yes* to his two-hundred-year plan, choosing to deny himself and take up his cross and follow Christ.

Twenty years later, Pops and I still meet every week for lunch and Bible study. He helps me make wise financial choices, and I help him invest his money in the First National Bank of Heaven, where he can cash in one thousand years from now. He has traveled with Brice and me to Peru to feed the poor. He also joined Blake and me on a Skip1 trip to Haiti and the Dominican Republic. Kay and Pops are living out true religion and have generously given of their time and resources to "the least of these" all over the world.

Pops is certainly not perfect; he was just wise enough to realize his money couldn't buy him a seat in heaven and that he needed to say yes to the God who already paid the price on his behalf.

I have watched Pops follow more and more after God, and I have seen him possess more and more a peace that surpasses all understanding. Whenever I think I'm having a bad day, I drive straight up to visit Kay and her beautiful smile and ask myself, "What's your problem again, Shelene?"

Perspective is amazing. God's perspective is life changing.

Lord, help me see that my real worth is based on who I am in Your eyes, and not on my worldly successes. Help me see those who are hurting so I can show them the unconditional love You have shown me. Give me the boldness to share Your love and truth with those who come across my path. Amen.

THIRTEEN

Just Skip It

I was not looking to start a charity. Frankly, I think there are too many already. But with my experiences in Africa and images of real starving children freshly seared into my mind, I just had to do something. Doing nothing was just not an option.

My plan was not to start a charity but to produce a TV show. Sometimes our most carefully laid plans are not God's plans.

With my entertainment industry background, my experiences got me thinking about how I could really make a huge difference. What if we filmed a reality show that basically showed what I had just been through? What if we followed a typical American from a world of luxury to a world where people were desperate for their next meal just to keep them alive? That would be really interesting and powerful. I started brainstorming and created a reality show concept called "America Gives."

The show took a pampered American family who were nominated by their relatives (who felt they were too spoiled) to spend a week in a third-world country, living alongside and helping improve the living conditions of the poorest of the poor. The goal was to bring lifesaving changes to a village that desperately needed it. The show featured our dream team: a host, a master builder (jack-of-all-trades type), a doctor, a teacher, an engineer, and a humanitarian.

Instead of *Extreme Makeover, Home Edition*, I was thinking *Extreme Makeover, Village Edition*. Instead of "Move that bus!" I was thinking, "Land that plane!" as a C140 cargo supply plane is landed, bringing urgently needed food, books, and medicine into a deserving location. We were not wanting to Americanize these villages but instead wanting to allow their natural environments to thrive with better living conditions, better school environments, and better health care.

The viewers would watch as an affluent family falls in love with the children and families who live in these villages. Imagine their reaction as they bring running water to a village for the very first time. Or the emotional impact when a lifesaving surgery is performed only because they were there to bring the help.

The best part of the show for me was that the viewers at the end of every episode could pick up the phone and call or text to donate money to the particular village they were watching on TV. I figured America is already programmed to call in and vote for shows like *American Idol, Dancing with the Stars*, and *The Voice*. How amazing would it be if we could tap into that technology and viewers could hit the number 5 and send five dollars to sustain a village with food and water? Americans could literally change the world one week at a time from the comfort of their living room couches.

The other cool thing about TV for me was that viewers could also see where their money was going. No more wondering if your donation was being wasted—you could see it in action every week. Everyone I told about the show thought it was an amazing idea.

After working and reworking the elements of the show and calling in some Hollywood favors, we got a pitch meeting with a major television production company, which produces shows that are household names. Their offices were located in the heart of Beverly Hills and were very impressive.

On our first meeting I met with a senior high-level executive in charge of development. She is young, beautiful, and super smart. I told her my story and pitched the show to her. To my surprise she absolutely loved it. She told me she would share it with her team and get back with me. After a couple of weeks, she called.

"Shelene, are you sitting down?"

"No. Why?"

"Because we're in. We love the show and want to set up pitch meetings with our contacts at the networks."

I covered the phone with my hand and screamed.

We put together a sizzle reel that was a small taste of the show. With the production company's name and reputation behind the show concept, we started setting up meetings to pitch it to the major networks: ABC, NBC, and CBS.

I was freaking out because these were not just ordinary Hollywood pitch meetings, these were meetings that could really make a difference. The day arrived for our first pitch, and after being covered in prayer by friends and family, I headed out the door to enjoy my favorite thing, the L.A. traffic on the 101 freeway on my way to Hollywood.

I had nothing to be nervous about. The heads of these networks were impressive, but God kept reminding me that I knew their Creator: *Him.*

As I walked into our first network pitch meeting, I felt very confident. I was surrounded with a team of industry movers and shakers. I was introduced and shared my story—how I went to Africa to see if my sponsored kids were real. Then I broke directly into the show pitch.

After I completed my story and pitch, we put in the sizzle reel. It all was perfect. I could see the execs on the edge of their chairs, fully engaged. When the video ended, the network executives started asking rapid-fire questions. They were very interested. They all were moved and said they would have their accounting people go over some of the budget issues with us.

I left on cloud nine, just knowing that we were about to solve world hunger. I figured if 50 million votes came in to *American Idol* each week to vote for the next rock star, imagine what might happen if they could literally save the life of a kid whose story they had just watched? If everyone just pushed 1 to donate a dollar once a week, that would be more than 50 million dollars a week. My brain was racing with the possibilities. I just knew this was God's plan to feed the children I had made that promise to.

Over the next few days, I was besieged with never-ending phone calls. Were vaccinations needed for the crew? Were there any locations closer than Africa? Did we have local contacts already on the ground? Could we do this with two, not three, camera crews? Could we guarantee enough needy locations for a few seasons? Yes, yes, yes, yes, and most certainly yes. Things could not be going better.

Then the call came from our development executive.

"I have some news for you."

My heart jumped. This was the moment I had been waiting for. "What? What? What is it?"

"They passed," she hesitantly said.

"What?" I was stunned. "But . . . they loved it."

"I know," she said. "They did, and they loved you and your story, but they're concerned that people in America don't really care about what's happening in the rest of the world."

Wow! I thought. *Doesn't the Bible say to go into "all the world"?* Yes, it does. The Bible also says narrow is the road that leads to life, and few find it. Apparently Hollywood hadn't found the road yet.

Our executive then said not to worry, we still had a few more networks to hit.

"Great," I said, thinking that first network had just made a *huge* mistake. *They will be kicking themselves when one of their competitors picks up the show and it goes through the roof.*

Our meeting with the second major network, like our first meeting, was great. This meeting was similarly as amazing as the first pitch meeting. The following day we met with the last of the big three networks.

A couple of weeks went by and once again the development executive called and said, "Well, it looks like one might be interested, but the other passed."

As our team took a second meeting with the network, the interest was still high. As the budgets were computed and the cost of worldwide production was considered, eventually that network passed too.

I couldn't understand it. I couldn't help but ask God, "Lord, what was that all about? Why did You have me walk into all those networks and pitch this idea that You placed on my heart if it was going to be a *Big Fat No*?"

Then a series of thoughts came into my heart and mind.

"Why did I have Moses go back to Pharaoh ten times to say, 'Let my people go'?"

"Why did I have Joshua and the Israelites march around the walls of Jericho seven times before I dropped them?"

"Why did I have the leper dip himself under the water seven times before I healed him?"

"Why did I anoint the shepherd boy David as king of Israel and make him a rebel for fifteen years before he ever sat on the throne?"

I have since come to understand the reality that sometimes God wants us to go through a process *without* ever achieving what we thought was the goal.

God cares about the journey more than the end result.

After much questioning and prayer over this, I felt as if the Lord was saying, "Shelene, I don't need a network TV show to feed My children. I used only five small loaves of bread to feed five thousand people. I just need *you* to say yes when I call and to be found faithful with the assignments I give."

God, was this experience really just all about me? Did I really just go through all this work and an emotional roller coaster because You never wanted a TV show to feed Your children?

Okay, Lord. I absolutely don't understand why You would not green-light this show, but I will just follow Your lead, and, yes, I will be ready for anything.

Sometimes I can get so excited to do something that I'll bust a wall down in the name of Jesus. Then God kindly points out the door that He had already placed for me to walk through. Oops.

God says, "My yoke is easy and my burden is light" (Matthew 11:30).

Still, I felt that God did not want me to just drop the idea of extreme village makeovers. Just because there would be no TV cameras filming the transformations, that did not mean we could not change the villages anyway. What if we did this on our own?

What if we challenged people to just support our cause out of their own excess? What if we got everyone on the planet to skip one thing once in their lives—a bottle of water, a manicure, a latte, a pack of gum—and take what they would have spent and donate that money instead to feed starving children? What if we started a website community and asked people to skip something they don't really need and give the money they would have spent to help these kids?

We could do our own, self-funded "America Gives," not as a TV show but as a way to feed the needy.

Yes, yes, God, that is exactly what we will do.

With that, Skip1.org was born.

If I was going to start a charity, I felt strongly that God was pressing on me three important things. First, I was to put no other name before God's. Skip1.org would have no celebrity names before it. It's not Shelene's Skip1. And unlike many charities, we would not seek celebrity endorsements. If celebrities came to volunteer, we would accept them like anybody else, but we would never seek out someone because he or she is famous.

Second, we needed to take away every possible barrier to giving, like the skepticism I had of charities. I was convinced that 100 percent of all our publicly donated funds needed to go directly to getting the food to children and to our projects.

Third, ask no one for money.

"What? God, how can I have a charity and ask no one for money?"

"*Just share your story, and I will open up the floodgates of heaven and pour out so many blessings that you can't contain. I own the cattle on a thousand hills. You are My daughter, Shelene. That makes you the daughter of the King. Daughters and sons of the King of the universe aren't running around asking for money. The Lord will be your provider.*"

On September 1, 2009, we launched Skip1.org. When God brought the idea of Skip1.org to my heart, I believe the Lord was saying, "*You're already doing* America Gives *on a personal level. You have been traveling to villages since 2003. Now just give others the opportunity to skip something and feed a child in need.*"

The reality is, when everyone skips, those little tiny sacrifices really do count. Your small sacrifice just might be the difference between a child living and dying. I hope you will visit Skip1.org and help us change the world one skip at a time.

Love is an action, *skipping* counts, and God wants us to *jump* all in.

Are you ready to say *yes* to God and love, skip, and jump your way into the plans He has for you? It may not turn out the way you thought it would. It didn't for me. But in the end God's plan will be revealed and the journey will be worth it, I promise.

Lord, give me the eyes to see what You would have me see through the processes You take me through. Remind me that sometimes You are more interested in the character built from the process than the results of my efforts. Help me identify the assignments You want me to take on. Help me remember that every skip for the sake of someone else—no matter the size—matters to You, because You draw the line at my heart. Amen.

FOURTEEN

The Bankrupt Rich

Just then a man came up to Jesus and asked, "Teacher, what good thing must I do to get eternal life?"

"Why do you ask me about what is good?" Jesus replied. "There is only One who is good. If you want to enter life, keep the commandments."

"Which ones?" he inquired.

Jesus replied, "'You shall not murder, you shall not commit adultery, you shall not steal, you shall not give false testimony, honor your father and mother,' and 'love your neighbor as yourself.'"

"All these I have kept," the young man said. "What do I still lack?"

Jesus answered, "If you want to be perfect, go, sell your possessions and give to the poor, and you will have treasure in heaven. Then come, follow me."

When the young man heard this, he went away sad, because he had great wealth.

Then Jesus said to his disciples, "Truly I tell you, it is hard for someone who is rich to enter the kingdom of heaven.

Again I tell you, it is easier for a camel to go through the eye of a needle than for someone who is rich to enter the kingdom of God."

When the disciples heard this, they were greatly astonished and asked, "Who then can be saved?"

Jesus looked at them and said, "With man this is impossible, but with God all things are possible." (Matthew 19:16–26)

As proud as I am to be an American, I can honestly say growing up in Southern California put me at a disadvantage spiritually. To put it bluntly, I am convinced our culture has an obsession with luxury, comfort, and ease.

Many of us have hopped on the treadmill of success and have experienced chasing hard after material comforts. I have come to believe most of us, first and foremost me, need to adjust our thinking about who we view as rich. After traveling the real world, not the resort traveling I used to do, I have come to the conclusion that almost all Americans are rich. It's not enough that as Americans we can afford to buy this book, but the fact that we are educated enough to actually read it makes us rich. We need to reset our thinking about what it means to be rich.

On one particularly memorable African trip, we were headed by bus from Kampala north to Mweya to meet some pastors. Along the way, a ride that was a mere eight-hour trek on a dirt road, we saw a beautifully stocked fruit stand with a large spray-painted sign that read, VIP TOILETS. At this point in the trip, any old toilet sounded good to me so the promise of VIP toilets was a welcome sight indeed. I persuaded our bus driver to pull over, and I made my way directly to the owner of the fruit stand.

"Can I use your VIP Toilet?" I asked awkwardly.

He held out his hand, clearly indicating there was a price to pay for such luxurious VIP accommodations. I pulled out two dollars from my backpack and placed them into his hand. With a big smile he handed me a single thin padlock key. "VIP toiwet," he proudly proclaimed in broken English as he pointed behind the fruit stand to a leaning outhouse with a rusty tin roof, nestled between a dilapidated hay wagon and a few haphazard rows of wilted corn.

Grateful at this point for anything that even resembled a restroom, I bounded off. As I got closer and closer to the VIP toilet, it began to look a lot worse. Yes, there was a door, but it was weathered and had several holes from corrosion, wear, or perhaps from previously jilted VIP customers. The key I had been handed fit into a rusty old padlock that was hanging from a crooked galvanized lock hasp. As I opened the door to the tiny outhouse, I gasped.

The VIP toilet I had just paid two dollars for the pleasure of using was simply a deep hole dug into the ground. There was no protective paper, no seat, no pedestal, no porcelain, and no water. Just a hole and a piece of rusty rebar that sported a roll of white toilet paper and more than a few flies enjoying the VIP treatment. Lovely.

As I finished my VIP experience, I balanced myself to pull at the suspended toilet paper, but then the key I had so dutifully protected slipped from my hand and dropped right into the rather deep hole. My first reaction was to ponder how I could fish out the key by reaching down into the hole, but I quickly decided that was not a good plan. In the end, deciding I had only a few options, all of which were bad, I am ashamed to admit I became a runner.

Yes, I left that outhouse and made a beeline directly to our bus without bothering to inform my host of the location of the missing key. I have prayed many times since for forgiveness and that the poor man had a spare key.

After my VIP toilet experience, I was compelled to do some research about basic sanitation around the world. I was shocked to find out that according to the United Nations Human Development Report in 2006, 2.6 billion people lacked basic sanitation.[1] In other words, 43 percent of the people on this planet have no indoor plumbing. I had no idea. To the fruit stand owner, the fact that there were walls for privacy and a roll of toilet paper made his outhouse fit for a VIP. Never mind there was no toilet, water, or plumbing.

Worse yet, 18 percent of the world population does not have access to an improved water source. That is 1.26 billion people who must hand carry their untreated and often unsafe water in jugs, bottles, or containers to survive.[2]

In 2013, only 12 percent of the world population had a computer and only 8 percent had an Internet connection.[3] Does that surprise you? It surprised me.

Because we have running water, flushing toilets, constant reliable electricity, a computer, and a wireless connection, most of us never give a thought about those who don't. We have so much here in America. If we need water, we don't need to get up at 4:00 a.m. and hike five miles to carry twenty-five pounds of brown water back to our homes—like the kids I met in Uganda.

To the contrary, our water comes purified, safe and ready to drink directly out of our faucets with just a flick of a finger. Sometimes even flicking our fingers is too much effort and inferred sensors turn on our faucets when we place our hands under the spout. But even that is not good enough. We have to buy specially cleaned and filtered water, pristinely bottled for our ultimate convenience. And when we get bored with plain water, we can choose water that comes in twenty-five different flavors. Bubbly or flat. Filtered or mountain spring. Sugared or calorie free. In clear bottles or blue tinted.

According to the Miniature Earth Project, if you slept in a bed last night, keep your food in a refrigerator, and keep your clothes in a closet, like I do, you are richer than 75 percent of the entire world population.[4] Yet we walk around saying things like "I'm broke."

Sonya was a beautiful, nineteen-year-old mom I met in the Pomplona Alta barrio on the outskirts of Lima, Peru. Brice and I were returning to the city of Lima with our Jungle Ride team after delivering a tuk-tuk (a three-wheeled scooter car, the front half of which looks like a motorcycle and the back half like a small hatchback car) to a nearby pastor. We had decided to stop in an area that looked particularly needy to distribute some left-over food and toys we did not want to see go to waste.

As our van pulled into what looked like a haphazard temporary settlement, we were taken aback by several houses that appeared to be made from crates with nailed-on cardboard. One of the more robust structures in the settlement was a small mud-brick grocery store with a tin roof. I headed over to the little store to see if I could get something bottled to clear my dusty throat. That's where I met Sonya.

When I first laid eyes on Sonya, she was standing at the "checkout" counter, an upside-down wooden crate with a door nailed to the top. She had placed a few meager vegetables and a previously hanging plucked chicken on the "counter" and was having a discussion with what appeared to be a friend, another young shopper. I could see they were engaged in quite a serious conversation. Unfortunately, it was all in Spanish, so I had no hope of eavesdropping despite being within hearing range from anywhere in the tiny store.

Luckily, our interpreter, José Luis, had wandered over to the store after me. I made my way to him and asked what they were saying. I would normally not be so incredibly nosy, but I could tell from the body language of the girls that something was wrong. After listening briefly, José quietly whispered to me, "They're trying to put their money together to be able to afford what they need for dinner."

It became evident they did not have enough money when Sonya picked up the chicken from the counter to hang it back up with a few other chickens.

"José," I whispered, "tell them that God will provide for their groceries." He flashed a big smile and began interpreting.

Before I left on this trip, a friend had given me several hundred dollars. "Put this to good use," she had said, pushing the money into my hand. "You will know where to give it." Throughout the trip, I had been waiting for the right opportunity. This was obviously it.

"José, better yet, tell them both to get all the groceries they want."

As José began to explain in Spanish what I had said, the thankful smiles of relief that came across both girls' faces were priceless. The shopkeeper's smile was even bigger. Sonya stepped away from the makeshift counter for the first time to give me a hug. I could see that the counter had been concealing her considerable tummy. From the looks of things, she appeared to be days away from giving birth.

As the two girls picked up their overflowing bags of groceries, the van's horn blew to signal we were departing soon. I said good-bye with a hug and loaded into the van. Just as we were about to roll out, I saw that Sonya had put down her bags and run over to the van. She began tapping on the window. I called José over to interpret.

"She wants to know your name," he explained.

"My name?" I said over the van's starting engine. "Sure, tell her."

"Her name is Shelene," José relayed.

She leaned back, sticking out her pregnant tummy. "Shelene," she said as she pointed to her protruding bump.

José interpreted in a voice that cracked with emotion: "She is going to name her . . . her child Shelene." As the tears began to pour down my cheeks, I smiled and waved, and off we drove, leaving Sonya and her unborn baby, Shelene, ever-shrinking figures through the dusty back window of the van.

Sonya and her little family live on two dollars per day. She doesn't have plumbing in her house; her water comes from a spigot located at the end of her dirt street. She doesn't have a refrigerator or a closet or a computer or an Internet connection. She has never even heard of Steve Jobs or Bill Gates. But she has a soul and sometimes goes to bed at night hungry so her children can feel a little fuller.

The reality is that less than 1 percent of the world lives as well as the average reader of this book, and the majority of the world lives on two dollars a day or less. The first time I heard that figure, I remember thinking, *That is so weird. How can it be?* when actually I should have been thinking *we* are so weird. We are overfed and unconcerned and don't even recognize how rich we are.

You may be thinking, *So? What's the big deal? So the average American has more, much more, than the average inhabitant of this earth. So what?* I understand this thinking; after all, it is exactly how I thought for much of my life, that is, until I actually saw the faces of those dying.

Why should we care? Well, the answer is really twofold. First, it is our responsibility as Christians to care for the poor. Yes, it's one of the most common commands in the Bible. Here are my top 6 passages out of 168 in the Bible that reference the poor. I discovered these verses, some for the first time, after my first trip to Africa.

Those who give to the poor will lack nothing, but those who close their eyes to them receive many curses. (Proverbs 28:27)

"But when you give a banquet, invite the poor, the crippled, the lame, the blind, and you will be blessed. Although they cannot repay you, you will be repaid at the resurrection of the righteous." (Luke 14:13–14)

"They also will answer, 'Lord, when did we see you hungry or thirsty or a stranger or needing clothes or sick or in prison, and did not help you?' He will reply, 'Truly I tell you, whatever you did not do for one of the least of these, you did not do for me.'" (Matthew 25:44–45)

"Give generously to them and do so without a grudging heart; then because of this the Lord your God will bless you in all your work and in everything you put your hand to. There will always be poor people in the land. Therefore I command you to be openhanded toward your fellow Israelites who are poor and needy in your land." (Deuteronomy 15:10–11)

One person gives freely, yet gains even more; another withholds unduly, but comes to poverty. A generous person will prosper; whoever refreshes others will be refreshed. (Proverbs 11:24–25)

The generous will themselves be blessed, for they share their food with the poor. (Proverbs 22:9)

I had never been taught these verses were in the Bible. If we as Christians are trying to figure out what God wants us to do, I'd say a good place to start would be to read these six passages again. And if that's not enough, read the other 162 verses in the Bible about the poor.

I used to think that true religion was attending and serving at my church. That was wrong. Here is what the Bible says about true religion: "Anyone who sets himself up as 'religious' by talking a good game is self-deceived. This kind of religion is hot air and only hot air. Real religion, the kind that passes muster before God the Father, is this: Reach out to the homeless and loveless in their plight, and guard against corruption from the godless world" (James 1:26–27 MSG).

The second reason you should care about the poor is that a life only focused on material things will lead you to ruin.

For some reason having material riches tends to make us apathetic about spiritual things. This was the problem with the church at Laodicea. Jesus specifically directed John to write a letter to warn them of their apathy.

> So, because you are lukewarm—neither hot nor cold—I am about to spit you out of my mouth. You say, "I am rich; I have acquired wealth and do not need a thing." But you do not realize that you are wretched, pitiful, poor, blind and naked. I counsel you to buy from me gold refined in the fire, so you can become rich; and white clothes to wear, so you can cover your shameful nakedness; and salve to put on your eyes, so you can see. (Revelation 3:16–18)

These Laodicean Christians were very wealthy with earthly riches but were bankrupt in terms of spiritual riches.

Consider the testimonies of six men of great wealth:

- John D. Rockefeller: "I have made many millions, but they have brought me no happiness."
- W. H. Vanderbilt: "The care of $200 million is enough to kill anyone. There is no pleasure in it."

- John Jacob Astor: "I am the most miserable man on earth."
- Henry Ford: "I was happier when doing a mechanic's job."
- Andrew Carnegie: "Millionaires seldom smile."[6]

In chapter 4, I asked you to ponder the question, what is holding you back from really jumping in with your Creator? Hopefully you've had a chance to honestly answer that question. This is the story of what was holding me back from *jumping*.

Since we were first married, Brice and I had dreamed of building a custom home just the way we wanted it. I love the movie *Father of the Bride*, in which Steve Martin plays the doting father George Banks, who is having a hard time facing the fact that his little girl is getting married. The reason I love the movie isn't due to its cinematic mastery (note the sarcasm), but I absolutely love the look and feel of the house in that movie. We actually bought the movie so we could stop the DVD on the various house scenes.

One night I had Pops, who was going to be our architect and builder, sit through the movie with me. "I want it to be just like this," I said, pointing to the outside of the house.

"Okay, honey," he'd say. "Keep saving."

Consequently, when our friends were all buying houses in their twenties, we were still in a rental because we had a savings plan to pay cash for a piece of dirt so that we could have a custom house built on it. HGTV was our favorite TV channel, and we watched little else. At one point we actually had a subscription to *Architectural Digest* magazine, just to get ideas.

When the money in our savings account was reasonably close to what was required to buy the dirt, we started looking for the land. The land search was an all-consuming process. We were in no hurry, so we searched for just the right piece in just the right neighborhood. Eventually we purchased the property.

After four years of land shopping and two more years of design, city approvals, and construction, the day finally arrived—we were ready to move into our first home. I loved it. It came out just as I had hoped.

Having the dream of a custom home was not a sin. What mattered was the place it took in my heart.

Puritan Richard Baxter said, "When men prosper in the world, their minds are lifted up with their estates, and they can hardly believe that they are so ill, while they feel themselves so well."[7]

My problem was that my mind was "lifted up with" my little estate, and I was feeling pretty good about myself and my accomplishment. When God finally got my attention, He needed to do some surgery on my heart of pride.

Lord, thank You for the resources You have blessed me with. I recognize that You have placed me just where You want me to be and given me the resources You want me to manage for You. Help me recognize those in need, and help me identify how I can help them and point them to You. Help me not just look out for my own interests but also the interests of others. And help me not allow the wealth around me to distract me from what You want me to be about. Amen.

FIFTEEN

For Sale by God

In 2011, after coming back from a trip to Haiti, I was reading the parable about the rich young man who came to Jesus and asked, "What do I have to do to inherit the kingdom of heaven?" Jesus said, "Sell all your possessions and give to the poor, and then follow Me." The rich young man went away sad because he was of great wealth.

These verses really hit me, having just experienced being with the poor in the slums of Haiti. You see, I had never thought of myself as rich. I was certainly "comfortable," but rich? But comparing my house and position in this world to those of Haitian people with whom I had just spent a week, I had to admit that no objective jury in the world would say I was not rich. Compared with these people, I was loaded.

I began to think about what I would do if God asked of me what He'd asked of the rich young man: to sell everything. Would I really do it? Would I ever hear God ask me to do that? Probably not. I began to pray and asked God to search my heart.

Challenged by the whole thing, I talked with Brice. He was totally against it.

"Honey, because we did it right, our house payment is much cheaper than any comparable house we could ever rent."

"I know. It's not about the money; it's about my heart," I explained. "If God asked that of me, would I really be able to do it, or am I just like the young rich guy who went away sad?"

I read the parable of the rich man to Brice. We both knew what this house meant to me. The comfort it was to me. It had been our dream that became a reality. We had put in blood, sweat, and tears. From a financial standpoint, selling made no sense. We had low payments and lots of equity.

Then I began to feel a tug on my heart. What if we let God be our Realtor? What if we held out our house to God and said, "Okay, Lord, if You want to sell it, it's Yours to sell"? *If the Lord really is in this,* I thought, *then with all the social media outlets, we should be able to sell this house without an agent.* Brice definitely didn't want to go against anything God was doing, yet at the same time he felt we needed to take a few days to pray about it.

"Okay. Absolutely, we will pray," I said.

A few days later Brice came to me.

He explained that he believed God was in this because there was no other motivation we could possibly have. He also strongly felt God could bring someone to us who would be willing to buy the house, without a Realtor. It was going to be "For Sale by God." If God brought us a buyer, we would donate what would have been the Realtor's commission.

With that we started sprucing up the house for the sale. I took some beautiful pictures and then with Brice's blessing posted them on Facebook and other media outlets. The comments back were, "Are you crazy, Shelene?" and "You're going to 'skip' the house? Why?"

Gotta love friends. As if this decision were not hard enough.

Let me point out that God is not calling everyone to put their houses up for sale and give to the poor. There is nothing necessarily wrong with owning a nice home. It is not a more "spiritual" thing to do to downsize or to sell your possessions. Our financial decisions are between us and God and no one else. If God puts it on your heart to sell something, you need to listen to that. That's what was happening to me, and as hard as it was, I was trying to listen.

About a week later, Brice and I were invited to celebrate an "open house–company warming" party at our friends' web design company, Clover. Clover had just moved into its brand-new location, and the amazing build-out had just been completed.

At the party, Brice and I started looking all around the 15,000-square-foot office space. It was done right, totally modern, high-tech, and very cool. The place looked as if it were right out of a movie. We walked over to congratulate our friends Jim and Sherry Elliston.

Sherry cried out when she saw us walking toward her, "Oh my gosh, Shelene! I heard you were selling your house."

"Yes," I said. "'Skipping' it, actually." I briefly told her the story.

Sherry said, "I think we would love to buy it."

"What?" I said, laughing.

"I absolutely love your house, and Jim and I want to move near your area to be closer to the company."

"Let's hook up next week," I said.

"Perfect," she said. "Can't wait."

I can, I thought.

As we were leaving the party, I looked at Brice with disbelief. "Are you kidding me? This is crazy. Do you think she is serious?"

"I guess we will find out next week, won't we?" Brice said.

"Shelene," he continued, "I know we both love Jim and Sherry, but we're not going to give our house away. We need to get a fair price."

"Of course, honey," I said.

The following week, just as planned, Jim and Sherry came over to see the house. They had been over before to hang out—even for Christmas Eve one year—but this time was different, they were potential buyers. We walked them through all the ins and outs of our home. We talked price that night because I wanted to scare them off. They said they wanted to take some time to pray and sleep on it.

"But just so you know, we are very interested," Jim said.

Great. Take all the time you need, I thought as the reality of the sale was hitting me.

"Let's have dinner next week," Jim said. We all agreed.

When they left, I was filled with strange emotions. *Why do I feel so scared, so sad?*

As I began to analyze what I was feeling, I thought, *Wow, this must have been how that rich young man felt*. I began to think about what Jesus had asked the rich young man, and his response: "When the young man heard this, he went away sad" (Matthew 19:22).

It was a lot easier to read about somebody else being sad than being sad about my own stuff. This was *big*. I had always been so judgmental toward the rich young man, thinking, *Come on, rich guy; it's Jesus. Sell your stuff and get your inheritance in heaven.*

It sure was a lot different when it was my life and my faith being put to the test.

Before I knew it our we-wanna-buy-your-house dinner was here. I was having big reservations. Jim and Sherry shared how they definitely, positively wanted to buy our house and for the price we were asking (a fair price, but no small sum), but wanted to wait till January of the following year to close escrow (ten months away). After expanding their business they wanted to save a bit of money to put as much cash down as possible. We had no problem with that, and we all agreed to move forward with the sale.

Brice said he'd draw up the agreement. It is nice having a lawyer for a husband to take care of little details like that.

I must admit I was blown away by the miracle of the whole thing. Did God really sell our house just like that? No Realtor, no hassle, no lockbox, no strangers coming in and out of my home, and, wonderfully, no commission. But I was starting to feel a bit uncomfortable. Okay, a lot uncomfortable. Where were we going to live now? What were the kids going to think? It was all happening so fast.

With that, the packing began. It was as if my house had cancer and I only had ten more months with it. Then the "lasts" started. The last Easter in the house. The last Mother's Day. The last kids' birthdays and the last team parties. Finally, the big one—the last Christmas.

I threw a couple of garage sales. "Skip your stuff, feed a child" was my slogan. I told the garage sale customers, "If you need it, take it. If you just want it, you have to buy it."

Everything went so fast. Since I knew we were downsizing, I sold or gave away massive amounts of stuff.

I started boxing up cabinets and photo albums and looking for rental houses. I have to admit I was in mourning big-time over my home.

I started to think about why I was feeling such a loss. I came to the conclusion that I really thought the house belonged to me. The right attitude would have been that it was truly the Lord's. God had provided us with the resources to get into that house, but those resources were His. We were just managing His money.

That was not my attitude. After looking, planning, building, and enjoying my house, that "possession" had begun to own me. Living in a rental was so much easier for me because I knew what was to come. I saved and saved, not buying or fixing up anything in the rental house because, to be honest, it wasn't my home. It was the landlord's. If he wanted to upgrade, he could pay for it.

My eyes were set on what was to come—my modest dream home. But now that we were selling, we could go back to renting a home, and I could just wait for my mansion in heaven.

Randy Alcorn describes in his book *Money, Possessions, and Eternity* an interesting observation from an American missionary who had been out of our culture on the mission field for many years. This missionary was returning to the field after a year's furlough and was asked, "What struck you the most in the time you were home with us?"

His matter-of-fact reply was sobering: "What struck me the most was how people use their houses to make statements to each other; their houses aren't just places to keep warm and dry, but showcases to display their wealth and impress each other."

Alcorn went on to say the sad thing was that if the missionary "had stayed in the United States for another year or two, he might no longer have noticed. Like the frog that boiled to death by degrees, we tend to gradually acclimate to our materialism, becoming desensitized to it. Finally, we regard it as normal rather than an aberration."[1]

After Thanksgiving, the move-out time for us was approaching fast. One day Jim and his business partner, Ben, were asking me about Skip1.org.

I shared with them how we were in the process of taking a site visit to raise money for a new kitchen in Lima, Peru, and they generously offered to donate a match grant. For every dollar skipped, Clover would match up to fifteen thousand dollars. Jim also asked if he could go with the Skip1 team to Peru and check it out. I said, "Absolutely," and off they went.

While Jim was traveling with our team, he visited the orphanage in Chilca, where the proposed kitchen and dining room were to be built. Jim was rocked by the needs of the kids and people he saw and met in Peru. When he got back, he and Sherry decided to build a home for a family Jim had met in Lurin.

Prudence and wisdom tell us to save up for emergencies and to put money away for retirement. Live the good life. That's what Americans call success, right?

What has changed for people like Jim and Sherry is they have stopped ignoring the children and families around the world who are dying from lack of clean water and food—*that*'s an emergency. When we see someone in need or dying, the emergency of that situation does not go away just because we choose to ignore it. God has allowed us and assigned us to live here. It's not all about us and our own. It's actually all about Him and His desires for our lives. Jim and Sherry went on to build the home for the sweet family in Peru.

Their company, Clover, also helped raised more than thirty thousand dollars with their match-grant idea and helped build the kitchen and dining room in Chilca.

God wasn't done with the Ellistons—or the Bryans, for that matter. After returning from Peru, Brice and I received word from Jim and Sherry. In a beautifully crafted e-mail they said, "We love your house and want to buy it, [but] Sherry and I both had a totally unsettled feeling about the decision. After praying and talking through the decision over the past couple weeks, we've decided to head a different direction with how much we are willing to spend on our next home. We feel if we skip getting exactly what we want just because we can afford it, we could free up funds to be more generous to others."

Wait. Are you getting this? The American dream says the only reason you'd leave the house you're in is to buy a bigger one. Even if you go into debt to do it.

Jim and Sherry had followed all the financial advice. They waited till they had the funds and weren't going to be upside down if they bought our home. I'm certain even Suze Orman would have thought they were making a great financial move. Jim and Sherry realized that it wasn't about whether they could afford it. It was about where God wanted them spending His money.

Jim wrote in his e-mail to us: "So, although we love your space, we are going to sadly have to pass on it. We both feel strongly that the Lord wants us to sacrifice this in order to do and give more over the next few years."

Wow! Making deposits in heaven, where we can cash in one hundred, two hundred, three thousand years from now, is never a bad idea. Fix your eyes on things above, not on earthly things. Please don't misunderstand me. Nothing is wrong with a nice house. It becomes a problem when you aren't willing to lose it.

I recently heard a story about African hunters trapping monkeys. These clever hunters hack a coconut in half and hollow it out. In the upper half of the hard shell, they drill a hole just big enough for a monkey's hand to pass through. Then they place a small, ripened orange in the other coconut half and fasten the two halves together. Finally, they tie the coconut to a tree and retreat into the jungle, to wait.

In time an unsuspecting monkey discovers the coconut containing the sweet-smelling orange. The monkey slips his hand through the small hole, grasps the orange, and tries to pull it through the hole.

Of course, the orange won't come out; it's too big for the hole. The persistent monkey struggles to pull and pull, but he keeps his fist wrapped around the orange and will not let go. He simply refuses to let go of his prize, never realizing the danger he is in.

While the monkey struggles with the orange, the hunters run in, throw a net over the monkey, and capture him.

Many of us are like that monkey. We think our stuff is so valuable we keep holding on with clenched fists. Until we are willing to put our stuff down and truly come before God with an honest, pure heart, we are missing out on what God is trying to give us. It's not until we open our hands, which releases the stuff we've been holding tightly, that He can place in them what He's trying to give us. Open hands come from an open heart. The truth is, a lot of us, myself included, like our stuff. We think it is worth something.

After going through this experience, after much prayer and reflection, we concluded that this was less about selling our house than being able to hold our home loosely, coming before God with totally open hands. We now have the privilege of renting our own house—at least that's how we think of it. God is the landlord, and we are just passing through, with our eyes fixed on what is to come. And just to avoid the monkey trap, Brice and I agreed that we would always keep our house up for sale: For Sale by God.

Lord, everything I have is truly Yours to do with what You wish. I surrender it all to You. I come before You with open hands, placing my life and my possessions at Your service. Guide me to where You want me to put Your resources. Give me the wisdom to invest in things with eternal value. Give me the strength to not get caught up in the frenzied materialism of my culture, and help multiply whatever I have to help those who are hungry and in need. Amen.

SIXTEEN

Divine Appointments

Our son, Blake, was turning thirteen in a couple of months, and one day, out of the blue, said, "Hey, Mom, can I skip my thirteenth birthday and go with Skip1 to Haiti?"

In response to this unexpected request, I wanted to say, "That's very sweet, honey, but *are you out of your mind?* No. Absolutely no." Despite the mental hissy fit that was going on inside my head, what calmly came out of my mouth, was, "Sweetheart, this is just a site visit to check things out to see if Skip1 is going to get involved with any projects in Haiti. Maybe next time, son."

"Don't you think you should pray about it first, Mom, and maybe talk with Dad?"

Don't you just love when your kids hit you in the heart with truth that you don't want to hear?

"Sure. Yeah, I'll do all that, but my answer, Blake, is no. I'd really like to check things out first."

"Okay," Blake said, "but I've been praying about this, and I'd really like to skip my birthday and help the poor. I am going to pray that God will change your heart, Mom." With that, he gave me a big hug, and he was off.

Ugh. Really, God? I don't need to pray about this, and I certainly don't need to talk with Brice. My twelve-year-old son is positively not going to Haiti. He's just a child. These trips can be dangerous and uncomfortable. I really don't think he should be exposed to all that suffering at such a young age.

Realizing that Blake would probably talk to his dad about wanting to go to Haiti, I knew I should get to Brice first. I figured it wouldn't be too hard to convince him to be on my side about keeping Blake stateside, given the safety concerns.

The next day when Brice got home from the office, I made dinner (cooking is not my strongest skill but I have a few go-to dishes that are hard to screw up). I made sure he was very comfortable in his favorite leather chair with a nice big glass of sweetened ice tea. When all seemed just right, I made my move.

"So, honey, you know my Haiti trip is coming up in a few months. We are going to some very dangerous parts of Haiti. We will be going to an orphanage that caters to children who are victims of AIDS."

"Why do I feel a setup coming?" he asked sharply.

Darn. Am I really that obvious? I was kicking myself for making dinner instead of my usual reservations—that was a dead giveaway. Brice, whose law practice concentrates on civil litigation, has been trained and is well practiced at sniffing out deception.

"So what's this about, honey?" he asked.

"Well, Blake came to me yesterday and said he wants to skip his birthday and go with me to Haiti and help the poor. I just don't think he should go. That place is hazardous."

He looked me right in the eyes and with disbelief in his voice announced without hesitation, "If our son, at twelve years old, wants to skip his birthday gifts and go help the poor, he is absolutely going. We are just going to have to trust that God will keep him safe."

"Brice, he's only *twelve*!"

"He is a young man, and you will be with him. Did you know that at twelve, future president John Quincy Adams went with his dad, John Adams, on a wooden sailing ship across the Atlantic Ocean in the treacherous waters of midwinter and was in a naval battle with a British frigate?"

I can always count on some historical lesson from my husband the history buff.

"And what year was that?"

"It happened to be 1778," he replied.

"Yeah, well, this is the twenty-first century, not the days of wooden underwear. And nowadays we can use our brains to keep us out of harm's way."

"Shelene, those kids in Haiti live in that environment every day, and most don't have a mama bear Shelene to look after them."

So much for getting Brice on my side.

Later that same week, my friend and highly awarded businessman Bill Herren began telling me about this amazing advertising agency he had just hired, Brandtailers. Bill explained that Cheril Hendry, the CEO of Brandtailers, was the genius behind the out-of-the-box advertising ideas that involved harnessing the power of social media. Bill was quite impressed with Brandtailers' work and was convinced Cheril and I should meet. He was certain Cheril could give some ideas on how to share Skip1 with the world. He was so insistent that I meet with Cheril he didn't even give me a chance to politely say no.

"Shelene," he said, "you absolutely have to meet Cheril. In

fact, I want you to come to my office this Thursday and you can meet her before our advertising meeting."

Bill was so enthusiastic it was clear he was not taking no for an answer. I agreed to come on Thursday.

When Thursday came around, I made the drive out to Bill's office. When I arrived, the receptionist informed me Bill was running late. She said, "Bill said to just go upstairs to the conference room and he will be joining you shortly."

As I entered the large conference room, a strikingly pretty blond lady sat alone at the head of the long, marble conference table. She stood up to meet me.

"You must be Cheril. I'm Shelene. I'm told Bill is running late."

"Yes, that's what I understand too. I just talked to him on his cell. He is adamant that you share your story with me."

"Well, sure." I proceeded to tell Cheril about my trip to Uganda in 2003 to meet my sponsored kids and about Skip1.org. She was listening with rapt attention.

After explaining the exciting things happening with Skip1, I told her how we were taking several trips to make some decisions about where Skip1 was going to be giving our support.

Upon hearing this she stopped me and said, "Shelene, my daughter, Erin, turns sixteen this year, and instead of a car or a vacation for her birthday, she really wanted to take a mother-daughter trip with me somewhere to serve the poor."

Really? Wow! She must be a remarkable girl, I thought. *I would have taken the car or the trip at sixteen.*

"Your daughter should meet my son," I said. "He wants to skip his thirteenth birthday and do the same."

Then I asked, "Why haven't you girls gone anywhere before?"

Cheril explained that every time they had signed up to go on a trip, something would happen. Their trip would get canceled or their schedules would change.

"My trip to Haiti for a site visit is in a few months. You and Erin should join us."

I was truly just being polite and wondering where the heck Bill was.

Then Cheril said, "When exactly in the next few months are you going?"

"We leave October 26," I said.

"What?" Cheril said, disbelief in her voice. "Did you say October 26?"

"Oh, is that bad for you?" I asked.

"No, no, it's not bad at all. It's just that, well, October 26 just happens to be my daughter's sixteenth birthday."

Cheril's eyes welled up with tears, and in that instant I knew this appointment we'd made, with a guy who never showed up, was never meant to be a business meeting at all. This was truly a divine appointment. Now *my* eyes were welling up.

Cheril said, "Shelene, I barely know you, but you know what? Erin and I would absolutely love to join you on that trip to Haiti."

"I would love nothing more," I replied. And I knew in my heart that Blake would be joining us on an adventure to Haiti too.

Little did I know the remarkable journey God had in store for Cheril and me, a journey that would go far beyond our trip to Haiti. Little did I know that not only would this trip rock us to the core but that Cheril as a future Skip1 board member would become one of the biggest champions of Skip1, with both time and treasure.

As our trip drew near, I felt myself becoming anxious about

this adventure to Haiti. Not about going to a third-world country—I had been to lots of underdeveloped counties—but about the adventure of taking my only son with me. On past trips he had always been safe at home with Dad or other family. Fear and anxiety began to set in.

I turned to the Scriptures to help me through. A lot of great verses I knew came to mind: "For I am the LORD your God who takes hold of your right hand and says to you, Do not fear; I will help you" (Isaiah 41:13). "Be strong, do not fear . . . he will come to save you" (Isaiah 35:4). But one verse in particular kept coming to my mind: "Do not be anxious about anything, but in every situation, by prayer and petition, with thanksgiving, present your requests to God" (Philippians 4:6).

I was really taking this one to heart, making my requests to God, all right. Requests like, "God, can You please make Blake sick so he doesn't have to go?" Of course, Blake stayed as well as well could be. He didn't even get a runny nose.

I finally realized that God is big enough and powerful enough to take care of my son. My failure to recognize that was the pinnacle of arrogance. I ultimately turned the whole thing over to God. Blake was going to be on this trip one way or another. I might as well start embracing it.

October 26 arrived and our Skip1 team met up at Los Angeles International Airport for our flight to Santa Domingo. Everything I had learned about Haiti in preparing for the trip helped me realize it was not the place to stay the night. It's weird how a little island in the Caribbean, Hispaniola, is shared by two countries. Haiti occupies the western one-third of the island, and the Dominican Republic is on the eastern side.

We decided our team was going to stay on the Dominican

Republic side and go into Haiti during the day, exiting the country before the gates of the city closed in the evening. We had made arrangements to hook up with our local connection, Esperanza, at the airport. Esperanza, which means "hope," is a nonprofit ministry founded by former major league baseball player Dave Valle.

After meeting with our Esperanza local connection at the airport, our team checked in to the hotel and turned in for the night. I couldn't wait to see what the Lord had planned for the morning.

The next morning Blake was the first one up in our room. He was dressed and ready to go even before I was out of the shower. We joined the others for breakfast and then boarded a bus to hit the poor villages of the Dominican Republic.

Our host and interpreter, Jean-Pierre, began to tell us about the first village we would be visiting. He explained that the orphanage at our first stop was filled with babies and children with AIDS. Soaking up every word Jean-Pierre said about the AIDS kids, my mind was racing in overdrive.

Does Blake understand what AIDS is? Does he have any cuts on his hands? I hate how that boy bites his nails all the time. Could he have opened up tiny cuts on his hands by biting his nails?

I wanted to warn Blake of the danger, but just then the bus began to slow as we neared the orphanage, and I realized I was all the way in the back of the bus and he was way in the front.

Should I get up and push my way to the front before Blake gets off to make sure he is aware of the danger?

Before my thoughts could shut up, I realized we were stopped and there was just not going to be enough time for me to make it to the front of the bus before the bus doors opened. I was panic-stricken as Blake was the first one to step out of the bus. I could only stare helplessly through the bus window, trying to act calm as I saw him beeline toward a group of orphans. It was all I could do to not push over every single person who came with our group.

I felt as if I were trapped in a traffic jam on the 101 freeway. There, stuck standing behind twelve other people, I watched out the bus window as my adolescent son scooped up a tiny little girl and began to laugh and love on her. As the people traffic jam finally let up, I quickly ran around the front corner of the bus, still desperate to inform Blake of the dangers.

Panic must have been all over my face as Blake said, "Mom, isn't she just the cutest thing?"

"Yes, of course," I answered.

Then, as if he could read my mind, he said confidently, with a knowing smile, "Mom, I know what AIDS is."

"Well, you bite your nails all the time," I answered. But Blake's smile grew wider and wider until he began to laugh. I couldn't help but join in.

Okay, Lord. I was a little over-the-top on this one. I am giving him over to You.

After finishing at the orphanage and the nearby village, we headed back onto the bus to visit a village in the Dominican Republic that is 90 percent Haitian immigrants. Jean-Pierre told me about a Haitian pastor who was ministering to this transplanted Haitian community. We pulled up to the church and were greeted by the pastor. Jean-Pierre made all the proper introductions in multiple languages. Why hadn't I stayed in French or Spanish class? It sure would have made things a lot easier.

We broke up our team into groups. Cheril and her daughter,

Erin, Blake, Grandpa Al, and I went with Jean-Pierre. We began to walk through a transplanted Haitian barrio with a hodgepodge of makeshift structures, some of unfinished rough concrete blocks, others of haphazard tin siding, and still others of broken and weathered plywood scraps. We approached a house that had walls made of wooden pallets. The house had a tin roof, a dirt floor, and no electricity or running water.

As we walked up to deliver food, a sweet young woman with two small children clinging to her legs opened the door. She welcomed us into her home. The entire house was ten-by-sixteen, a little smaller than my bedroom.

With Jean-Pierre interpreting, I asked, "Are these your children?"

She responded in Caribbean French. "Yes," Jean-Pierre interpreted. "She has three children: these two and a thirteen-year-old daughter."

"Really? Where is she? I'd love for her to meet my thirteen-year-old son and Cheril's sixteen-year-old daughter."

As Jean-Pierre started translating my words, the mood in the tiny shack changed quickly. Even though I had no idea what the heck they were saying, I knew something was wrong. It's amazing how a mother's bond transcends language. As tears began to fill this young mom's eyes, tears also began to fill Cheril's and mine. Jean-Pierre began to share this woman's desperate story.

She had been born in Haiti. When the economy collapsed, she was in a very difficult and desperate situation. Her young family was struggling for each and every meal. They were lucky to get one meal a day. They were basically starving and dehydrated from the lack of food and clean water.

In her desperation, this woman had to make a decision that

moms like me will never have to make. In her hopelessness she had made the reckless decision to sell her oldest daughter to save the others.

"Well, where is she? Let's go get her," I said with urgency in my voice.

Jean-Pierre shook his head. "Her daughter is in Haiti, but she has no idea where."

At that moment, I completely lost it. I grabbed the woman and hugged her as if my hug could bring her daughter back. Tears were streaming down our faces as we embraced. The pain of that moment, the shame and guilt, was a weight she could no longer bear. But she had two little daughters who were alive standing next to her. I was thinking about the innocence of my own daughter back home.

In this book, I will refer to this mother as Elowese. She is one of the reasons I fight every day to bring food and clean water to families in need. Never again do I want a mother like Elowese to be forced to make such a gut-wrenching decision.

Later, we boarded the bus to head back to our hotels for the night. I don't think I spoke a single word the entire ride back.

Lord, I am no better than this mom. Why was I born in America, and she was born here with no opportunity? Why did You have me meet her today? Questions were coming faster than I could think of answers. To this very day Elowese's picture hangs in my home office, framed by my dear friend Cheril Hendry as a reminder to never take my eyes off the poor.

One of the most jarring teachings Jesus ever gave offered a vivid description of an epic day in the future—Judgment Day. This is a day when "all the nations," every person from all time, will be gathered together before the throne of God. Jesus' teaching gave us a strikingly clear picture of God's attitude about us taking care of the "least of these" (Matthew 25:40), the poor.

In Matthew 25:31–34, Jesus describes the scene on Judgment Day:

> "When the Son of Man comes in his glory, and all the angels with him, he will sit on his glorious throne. All the nations will be gathered before him, and he will separate the people one from another as a shepherd separates the sheep from the goats. He will put the sheep on his right and the goats on his left. Then the King will say to those on his right, 'Come, you who are blessed by my Father; take your inheritance, the kingdom prepared for you since the creation of the world.'"

In verses 41–46, we see God's disgust with those who ignore the poor.

> "Then he will say to those on his left, 'Depart from me, you who are cursed, into the eternal fire prepared for the devil and his angels. For I was hungry and you gave me nothing to eat, I was thirsty and you gave me nothing to drink, I was a stranger and you did not invite me in, I needed clothes and you did not clothe me, I was sick and in prison and you did not look after me.'
>
> "They also will answer, 'Lord, when did we see you hungry or thirsty or a stranger or needing clothes or sick or in prison, and did not help you?'
>
> "He will reply, 'Truly I tell you, whatever you did not do for one of the least of these, you did not do for me.'

"Then they will go away to eternal punishment, but the righteous to eternal life."

Who are the "least of these" in our modern Western society? Well, those who don't have enough food to survive, those who don't even have access to clean water, those who don't have a bed to sleep on, no electricity, no indoor plumbing. I had encountered plenty of people and children like that in Haiti, but let's face it, most of us don't get there very often. What about here in America? On the streets of America, there is a substantial homeless population who are often despised by our whole society, even those who claim to love God. I have actually turned away from the homeless in disgust, thinking, *Just get a job*.

Let me challenge you to consider this passage very seriously. Do you think the words Jesus spoke here were lies? Do you think Jesus was joking when He said, "Whatever you did not do for one of the least of these, you did not do for me"? Have you ever looked at a homeless person and imagined the face of Jesus on that individual? That is actually how God looks at it.

If you're like me, after reading those verses you have to ask yourself, "What have I been doing for the 'least of these'?"

Lord, help me see my children as gifts from You that are not mine but Yours. Give me the strength to hold them loosely so You can grow them up to be people with hearts to serve You. Help me look upon the "least of these" with Your compassion and love. Give me the strength, energy, and passion to do whatever I can to feed the desperate and care for those who are abandoned. Amen.

SEVENTEEN

The Mailbox at Apartment #2

Let me just say it. I had an issue with homelessness. By "issue" I don't mean I wanted to help the homeless or somehow eradicate homelessness. Seriously, when it came to homelessness, I had absolutely no tolerance. I'd always thought, *People, you live in America, the land of opportunity. Do something. Get a job. Deliver pizzas on your bike. Anything but stand on a street corner with a begging can.*

I was a girl who had started my own business doing direct-market advertising when I was seventeen and went on to own several businesses. I had an enormous judgment problem. Uninformed and controlled by my unreliable stereotypes, I was certain that all homeless people were lazy, on drugs or alcohol, or just plain mentally ill. I loved serving, helping, and loving on the little children of the world, but the slightly greasy chick who stood outside of my Trader Joe's next to her shopping cart containing the sum total of all her belongings, begging for money, bugged me.

Several years ago I had an opportunity to speak at an event to a large group of businesspeople in Laguna Niguel, California. Author and popular motivational speaker Seth Godin was speaking after me.

That night I was moved by something Seth said. He asked, "When was the last time you did something for the first time?"

For some unknown reason, as I pondered Seth's question, the word *homelessness* popped into my head and would not get out. My thoughts were running wild, *Shelene, you say you are a Christian, but will you only love people who are on the other side of the world, or your neighbors who are well off and have homes?*

On my drive back from the Seth Godin event, the homeless lady outside my Trader Joe's plagued my thoughts. Finally, I burst out loud in the car, "Okay, God. If You want me to help some homeless people, You will have to make it happen. Drop them in my lap."

A few weeks later, Skip1 board member Cheril Hendry invited me to come to a lunch with social media guru and author Chris Brogan. Chris has written several books, including *Trust Agent* and *The Impact Equation*.

I arrived at Cheril's office and after introductions and pleasantries, Cheril asked if I could share my Skip1 story with Chris. I shared, and we instantly hit it off.

Chris said he'd love to help Skip1 any way he could. He loved the simplicity of our charity and my story. He then said, "Shelene, Skip1 reminds me of another charity I support, Invisible People. You absolutely have to meet Mark Horvath. I believe you two will become fast friends."

"Sure," I said, trying to be polite, "but what's Invisible People?"

"Oh, Mark helps homeless people by giving them a voice via webcast."

"How does that help them?" Was that my cynical outside voice?

"Well, he was once homeless himself," Chris explained,

"and he has a huge heart, like you, and YouTube actually has given him their home page to showcase the stories he shoots about homelessness."

"I'd like to meet him someday." I must admit this was not the full truth. I really had no desire whatsoever to meet somebody who was homeless or had ever been homeless. Feeling a bit uncomfortable but not wanting to show it, I just smiled, trying to think of how to change the subject.

"I am speaking at a business conference next month," Chris went on, "and Mark is going to be there. Why don't you come as my guest? I'd love to give a shout out to Skip1 and Invisible People."

Right. There is that homelessness thing again. Ugh. Really, God? Are You trying to get my attention? Okay, Lord. I am starting to get the message.

"Sure. Yes. I'd love to be there."

I had a suspicion this upcoming meeting was a direct result of my talk with God in the car after my Seth Godin "homelessness" moment.

That night I read Matthew 25:45–46, and once again, those now-familiar words of Jesus cut to my heart: "Truly I tell you, whatever you did not do for one of the least of these, you did not do for me."

I knew I had been taking care of the "least of these" in Africa and other parts of the world. But as I read that verse, a question came to mind: Who are "the least of these" in this country?

Well, God, if the homeless on the streets are not the "least of these," I don't know who would be. Okay, God. It's time for some open-heart surgery. You need to cut pride, judgment, and self-righteousness out of my heart.

That week I went to our Skip1 meeting all charged up. I explained to the board how God kept putting the homelessness issue in front of me. As it turned out, two of our board members, Matt Warren and Drew Lucas, were already huge fans and supporters of Mark Horvath and Invisible People. It certainly seemed as if God was trying to get my attention when it came to the homeless. I also explained how my own heart had been strongly rebelling against this homelessness thing. That needed to change.

I felt that Skip1 needed to get involved in partnering with Mark for a Skip1 homelessness event. Immediately the consensus around the room was, "Great idea! Let's do it." Meanwhile, I was wondering, *Am I the only one on the Skip1 board who has a problem with helping the homeless?*

Matt offered to reach out to Mark and set up a lunch. Just like that the yes ball was rolling.

Not long after, I decided to meet Mark at Path Achieve, the homeless shelter where he worked. I was extremely honest with him about my inaccurate thoughts and feelings regarding homelessness. Mark explained that in a small respect some of my thoughts were accurate.

"About 30 percent of homeless people are on drugs, abuse alcohol, or are mentally ill," he said. "Then there's another group, like those at Path Achieve, that just need a leg up. Men, women, and children."

With a single word Mark hit my heart with what seemed like a dagger.

"Children?"

"Yes, children. Shelene, right now we have about fourteen children, from three months to fifteen years."

My heart sank. "Really? And they live here?"

"Yes. Here in Glendale every guest has to be drug tested to get in. They are only allowed to stay for ninety days. Path Achieve gives them resources and a chance to get their dignity back."

Wow. I had no idea, and I had certainly never been to a homeless shelter before.

I shared my desire to do a "Skip for the Homeless" event near Christmastime. With the thumbs-up from Mark, Matt, and Drew, I made a call to secure a warehouse that our big supporters Jeff and Denise Sponseller owned and had offered for free for the event.

This event was the first of its kind. We blasted out to our Skip1 community our need for volunteers, and bam! Two-hundred-plus skippers signed up and turned out for our event.

I got an idea from Erin Hendry (then a sixteen-year-old world changer), who suggested we make G-love bags. "What's a G-love bag?" I asked.

She explained that they would be little bags that fit in your car's glove box, filled with things homeless people need. The bags would be like miniature backpacks with a drawstring, similar to the plastic Apple Store bags. "When you're out and about and you see a homeless person, you can reach into your glove box and hand them a G-love bag filled with love," Erin explained. I liked it.

I asked Mark what he thought we should put in the G-love bags. What he said surprised me.

"Be sure to put a pair of socks in there."

"Socks?"

"Yes, homeless people rarely get to change their socks. Think about it: they don't have a washing machine or dryer; they're homeless."

Got it. So socks it was.

"What else?"

"I think you should put in a rain poncho, lip balm, a bottle of water, a granola bar, and a small first-aid kit. Maybe gift cards for food."

Thanks to our sponsors, in addition to socks we bought all the items Mark had suggested. Our local McDonald's donated gift cards that would provide each homeless person a meal. We stacked all these donations on tables for the assembly line volunteers to get to work stuffing the G-love bags with all that good stuff. Everything was ready to go. Mark was set to speak, and the volunteers had arrived with joy in their hearts to do a good thing. Then it came time to start stuffing the bags. Everybody was having a blast packing them with love.

Once we finished stuffing the G-love bags, Mark got up and shared our surprise plan. The G-love bag delivery was not going to be done by Skip1 at all, but by the volunteers who had just stuffed them.

"That's right," he said. "We are so glad you all showed up today and filled these three-hundred-plus bags. But these bags are not for Skip1. They are for you to take home and put in your glove box to hand out to the next homeless person you see and find out their story."

Our purpose was for each volunteer to have a positive interaction with a homeless person.

It was amazing to observe the silence that blanketed the warehouse. The looks on some of the volunteers' faces were just priceless. It was clear that many shared my own discomfort with the homeless.

It's one thing to love; these volunteers gave of their time and served, putting love into action. It's another to skip; these volunteers skipped their Saturday to shine the light on the least of these. Skipping matters, but this event required us to jump in. Jumping, as many of you know, is much harder. I can get trained to skydive on the ground. I can even love the idea. I can leave the comfort of standing on solid ground and actually get in the plane. But I'm still not a skydiver until I jump.

When our event was over, we were driving home, and my daughter, Brooke, couldn't find a homeless person fast enough. With her back window rolled down and half of her little body hanging out the window, she yelled, "Mom, I see one! Merge over, Mommy."

As I pulled into the Office Depot parking lot, Brooke jumped out of the car and ran to the corner where an old homeless man held a sign: "Homeless. Please help. God bless."

Brooke greeted him as only a child can. "Hi. I'm Brooke. I have this G-love bag for you."

"Why, thank you," the sweet-faced man said. "What's a G-love bag?"

"It's a bag made with love for you."

A smile began to warm his face.

"May I open it now?"

"Sure," Brooke replied.

"Thank you very much."

"You're very welcome." With that, back in the car she jumped. Watching her joy and lack of fear humbled me.

That night, once again, I couldn't sleep. I was feeling a bit like a hypocrite, wanting all those volunteers to have a positive interaction with a homeless person, and yet I'd truly never had one myself. I started thinking . . .

Suddenly it hit me. *What would it look like if I opened up all my connections to one homeless person and gave them the leg up of a lifetime?* I knew someone who owned an apartment building in Van Nuys. I had friends who change their furniture whenever Pottery Barn or Restoration Hardware gets their new spring collection. I knew people who could help with a job. *What if? What if . . . I said* yes *to this crazy idea and jumped in?*

The first thing the next morning, I was on the phone with Mark.

"So, Mark, here's my idea. I was thinking, what if everyone took just one homeless person in their community and gave them the leg up of a lifetime? You must know someone at the shelter who needs a second chance."

Over the time I had been hanging around Mark, I had learned that many homeless people actually have some sort of job. Most just don't make enough money for first month's rent, last month's rent, plus the security deposit. Not to mention the other deposits or ability to pass credit checks to turn on water, power, and gas to get into an apartment. Most homeless don't have cars or access to a phone or the Internet.

I started calling my friends and family and explaining what I wanted to do. Then I took a drive out to the apartment building in Van Nuys.

Once there, I found apartment #2, unlocked the door, and walked in. It was a studio. It had just been repainted and was very clean, including new carpet. It had a full kitchen with a new refrigerator, and a large, walk-through closet that led to a full bath: tub-shower combo and everything.

It was perfect.

As I left the building, a feeling of complete joy came over me. I couldn't wait to call Mark.

"Mark, I was able to get an apartment basically at cost. Have you found anyone who needs an apartment and can handle six hundred dollars per month?"

"I have the perfect person, Shelene. Her name is Rd."

"What? Rd? How is that spelled?"

"The capital letter *R* and small letter *d*. Rd. I have been working with her to get a state grant for her security deposit and first month's rent. It looks like it might take a few more months."

"A few more months? That's crazy. The apartment is ready for her now. I don't feel right about keeping her on the streets for a few more months while we wait for all the bureaucratic paperwork to get done. Mark, let me call you back in a little while."

My next phone calls were rapid dial to the board members of Skip1. After a discussion we all agreed to skip the bureaucracy and get our new homeless friend Rd into apartment #2 immediately. "Let's get the water and power turned on. We will put up the first month's rent and security deposit."

At that moment the verses that had become so familiar to me came into my head: Matthew 25:37–40, and in particular, "Whatever you did for the least of these, you did for me" (paraphrased).

Of course, the scribes and Pharisees, who had failed God, defensively asked, "Jesus, when did we see You hungry and needing a place to sleep?"

Jesus replied, "Truly I tell you, whatever you did not do for one of the least of these, you did not do for me" (v. 45).

A chill went down my spine. I thought about my attitude over the years when it came to homeless people. They had unquestionably been considered "the least" in my mind. My thoughts expanded even more as I heard the verse play again in my mind: "Whatever you did for the least of these, you did for *me.*"

Was Jesus moving into apartment #2?

I started making calls to key people to see if we could round up some furniture. My friend Deb said, "Shelene, I can get some people to donate the furniture." Within forty-eight hours we had furnished the entire apartment.

The day finally arrived. I had a small group join me at the apartment to put on the final touches before Rd was to arrive. Deb and I could feel the excitement as our kids finished decorating the apartment. It was furnished with a sleeper sofa, a beautiful wood-and-glass coffee table, and a matching wood hutch that was used to hold the TV. Deb's friends had donated a round dining table with matching chairs. We had collected dishes, cups, plates, and silverware. Someone else had donated a desk with all the trimmings so Rd could continue her online job.

People donated brand-new, hotel-quality bath towels, washcloths, hand towels, shampoo, soap, toothpaste, and toothbrushes. The pantry was stocked with enough toilet paper and paper towels for a year.

The only thing missing was Rd.

As Mark Horvath, accompanied by Rd, pulled his van to

the curb outside the complex, we were standing there to greet her. As Rd exited the van, that tiny, five-foot-three lady was full of joy. Her face was lit up like a child's at Christmas. She pointed two fingers at me, and I rushed in for a celebratory hug and welcomed her to her new zip code. I could not help but feel like I was on an episode from HGTV.

I reached out to hand Rd the key to her new apartment. Taking it, Rd waved her arms over her head in a dance of joy. We headed through the glass doors into the foyer of the building. Rd's every step radiated with energy and excitement. Her grateful spirit was contagious. She was so thrilled and appreciative.

As we passed by the courtyard with the pool, she said, "Well, I haven't seen one of these in a while."

Looking ahead of me, I asked, "What? A swimming pool?"

"No, the mailbox," Rd said as she looked to her left, nodding at the bank of silver aluminum mailboxes hanging on the wall.

I was stunned. A mailbox? But, of course, it all made sense: Homeless people don't get mail. They don't have an address to call home. I'd never seen anyone excited about a mailbox until that moment.

As we approached the door to apartment #2, Rd held up her key with a slightly shaky hand from all the excitement and anticipation. She slipped it into the lock and turned the handle with a click. As the door to her new digs swung open, she was overwhelmed.

"Holy cow! Somebody moved in before I got here. Whoa!"

Not expecting furniture and thinking she was going to be sleeping on the carpet, she had been thankful just to have a roof over her head. Now she was completely shocked as she walked through her fully furnished new apartment and sat on her new couch. She was astounded as she opened cabinets full of goodies and realized that her bathroom had a tub *and* a shower.

Watching Rd's reaction, I was smiling so hard my teeth were drying. (You can watch Rd's reaction and see her apartment at SheleneBryan.com.)

It was as if I could once again hear God saying, *"Are you having fun yet, Shelene?"* At that very moment I can truly say there was nothing you could have bought me or a trip I could have taken or an outfit I could have worn that would replace that feeling of complete contentment. Doing something for someone who can do absolutely nothing for you in return is addictive.

My new friend was a sobering reminder for me to appreciate what I have. I had never even given a thought about my own mailbox. Whenever I get my mail now, I smile in a way I never have before. Whether it contains bills, junk mail, wedding invitations, or sweet Hallmark cards, I'll never take my mailbox for granted again.

Love lived out is rarely realized by just hanging out in a church. True love is an action. I challenge you to do something for someone who can do absolutely nothing for you in return. You won't regret it. As Jesus said, "Whatever you did for the least of these, you did for me."

It has been several years, and Jesus is still living in apartment #2. The rent has been paid faithfully every month—and always on time.

Lord, help me see and love those who are unseen and ignored. Give me Your deep capacity to love even if I don't want to. Help me see You in those who are poor, weak, needy, sick, mentally ill, and helpless. Help me love those who have been outcast and looked upon as nothing. Give me the strength to give someone a second chance. Amen.

EIGHTEEN

Throw It Off

A few years ago I was invited to speak at TEDx Orange Coast in Southern California (TED stands for Technology, Entertainment, and Design). One of my fellow speakers was a young guy named Sizhao "Zao" Yang.

Zao was a plain-talking, techy type who was obviously very intelligent. It was evident that speaking before enormous crowds was not his favorite thing to do, but he managed to put aside his fear and made a very interesting presentation.

After the event we exchanged business cards, and a few months later I met Zao for lunch in Santa Monica near his office.

Zao's story is crazy. He was born in China but grew up in Glenview, Illinois. He attended the University of Illinois at Urbana-Champaign, where he studied computer science, mathematics, and finance. After college he used his programming brilliance in the tech field to land a position at IBM. Within a year, he wanted something different. He applied to UCLA for graduate studies and came to Los Angeles.

Then he had a big idea: What if he could create games for use on social media platforms, like Facebook? Zao was convinced he could raise the quality of Internet games. He was very

185

interested in games where people became socially connected and emotionally involved. He recognized that people want to be seen and heard and to have a positive emotional experience with their social games. But games were not being designed to "hug" the user, and Zao wanted to tap into the power of our emotional needs.

The summer before starting his graduate program at UCLA, he founded a company called MyMiniLife. He and a friend drained their savings accounts and invested five thousand dollars each to start the company.

As time went on and he was dividing his time between UCLA and his start-up, Zao realized that his dream was going to die if he failed to put all he had into the project. He wanted to give all his energy and efforts to his gaming work, so, after much distress, he dropped out of UCLA. Zao's dad was understandably furious about his son quitting school and essentially cut him off. His family wouldn't listen to or support his gaming ideas.

After getting rejected by eight different investors, he left Los Angeles and moved to Silicon Valley. To make ends meet, he worked two part-time jobs, and he poured every moment of his free time into his start-up company. Despite the fatigue from working late into the night and getting up early, he kept going.

Zao decided to submit his game MyMiniLife to a tech review site called TechCrunch, which loved the game and provided a link to a mock-up version for their users to review. Suddenly things started going crazy.

"VCs (venture capitalists) woke up on Monday; they saw us on the site. Accel called me, Polaris Ventures called me, and two angel investors called me. I was this kid in San Mateo, and they e-mailed our customer support and said, 'Can you put me in touch with Mr. Yang?' I wrote back, 'Surely, I'll coordinate immediately.'"

Using the platform designed for MyMiniLife, Zao and his team developed the blockbuster social-media-based game called Farmville, where millions of Facebook users would build virtual homes with virtual goods. The Farmville platform was a phenomenal sensation, with 200 million users. Its progeny, Cityville and Frontierville, using the same platform, garnered a whopping 500 million users. Zao sold MyMiniLife in 2009 to Zenga for an undisclosed amount known to be in excess of one *billion* dollars.

It's so easy to celebrate this story, isn't it? We just love celebrating someone who goes after a dream and hits it big with the odds stacked against him.

Zao's story intrigued me. He was willing to throw off all that encumbered him to run toward something he was passionate about: to ditch tradition, sacrifice family approval, and run hard—not walk—toward his end game (no pun intended).

Zao decided to say *yes*. He was going to jump all in. It's easy in hindsight to say he chose wisely. Remember, though: Zao didn't have his Cinderella ending yet. He had no idea if he would be disowned, disgraced, and in debt. I'm not sure what Zao's spiritual beliefs are but his story reminds me of what our relationship with God should look like. Zao did something few Christians do: sacrifice everything for his goal.

Hebrews 12:1–3 says:

Therefore, since we are surrounded by such a great cloud of witnesses, let us throw off everything that hinders and the sin that so easily entangles. And let us run with perseverance the race marked out for us, fixing our eyes on Jesus, the pioneer and perfecter of faith. For the joy set before him he endured the cross, scorning its shame, and sat down at the right hand of the throne of God. Consider him who endured such opposition from sinners, so that you will not grow weary and lose heart.

If we are Christians, we have been given the power by the Holy Spirit to throw off all that encumbers us, the entanglements of this world, and run hard down the path God has set before us. We need to fix our eyes on the sacrifice of love God made by giving His Son so we can live our very best life.

It's so easy to let public opinion, fame, riches, and even our own families distract us from this pursuit. What's scary is, a lot of the time, we really don't care. We sometimes even use those distractions to put God in the backseat, or even the trunk, until we need to bring Him out to bless us or fix something that our money, fame, friends, or family can't.

We desperately need to run toward the path God has for our lives, even more than we know or believe. It is much easier to read that than to live it out. The titles or positions we have at work all too often define us. The awards we've received. The colleges we are attending or graduated from. The person we've dated or married. The talented kids we've raised. The family legacy we have. The fortune we will inherit. It's all meaningless, all distractions.

King Solomon wrote in Ecclesiastes about all he had learned in his life. His worldly pursuits were quite considerable: wisdom and knowledge, physical pleasures and wealth unmatched in the world at the time.

Yet at the end of his years, he boiled it all down to the crux of life: "And the dust returns to the ground it came from, and the spirit returns to God who gave it. 'Meaningless! Meaningless!' says the Teacher. 'Everything is meaningless!' . . . Now all has been heard; here is the conclusion of the matter: Fear God and keep his commandments, for this is the duty of all mankind" (Ecclesiastes 12:7–8, 13).

"Fear God and keep his commandments" was the instruction from the one who some say was the wisest man who ever lived.

In 2007, Brice and I traveled to Lima, Peru, to witness firsthand the impact Jungle Ride was having on the Children's Hunger Fund food pack program. The program was designed to bring transportation to support food pack networks. It was growing like crazy and had expanded from bicycles to tuk-tuks.

Our friends had donated one of these cars to CHF, and two other generous donors had provided the money for two more. We were going to be bringing these tuk-tuks to three well-deserving pastors who had demonstrated their faithfulness in administering the food pack program and who kept proper reports (always a challenge in cultures that see no need for records whatsoever).

We visited a church called Palabra de Vida in Chorrillos, Peru, to deliver one of the tuk-tuks. Pastor Faustino Mamano has one of the most infectious countenances I have ever seen. You could see that the man was at peace with his Maker. He laughed loudly and often.

Pastor Mamano took us to several homes of the poorest members of his congregation who were receiving food packs.

We had some amazing conversations with broken and grateful people as we passed out food and prayed with these families. As it started getting dark, we were anxious to wrap up our home visits due to safety concerns. It was not such a great idea for a bunch of unarmed gringos to be hanging around in the middle of a crime-ridden barrio at night.

We were just about to shut down the operation when Pastor Mamano, with desperation in his voice, practically begged us to visit just one more home. "I want you to pray for this old woman whose daughter faithfully attends our church." We could see that he was not going to take no for an answer.

"Okay," I relented. "But then we really must be going."

He led us down a dirt street, rutted and muddy from a late-afternoon rain shower, to a property that looked more like a junkyard collection of broken construction materials than a place where someone could live. As we drew closer, we realized that these various materials were banded together with a single strip of barbed wire in an apparent effort to keep a very thin goat from wandering off. The goat was tethered with a rope around its skinny neck, so it looked like the makeshift fence of half-rotten plywood, metal sheeting, and crooked branches was not very successful at keeping the elderly goat corralled.

As we approached the house, a beautiful woman in her sixties, with skin that looked like a thirty-year-old's, flung open the half-hung wooden door. This joyful lovely woman in her light-blue dress was such a contrast to the drab surroundings that it seemed as if she were backlit with rays of streaming light, like a scene out of the TV show *Touched by an Angel*.

She invited us in with her warm smile and kind, welcoming words. As we entered, I realized this was a one-room shack, separated by a large sheet to make what looked like a sleeping area behind the front living space. My attention was immediately drawn to the hard-packed dirt floors. If dirt floors could be clean, this floor was unquestionably the "clean dirt floor" winner.

It was dusk, and she had lit a tall candle and fastened it with melted wax onto an upside-down pot that she would normally use for cooking. We handed her a food pack box, which she accepted with a gracious smile. As she held the box of food, she explained that four generations of women lived here in her home. Then she walked over to a crude, two-by-four framed bed, where her frail, eighty-nine-year-old mother was lying under a blanket.

I was startled because although I had been standing only a foot from the bed, her mother was so small and inconspicuous I had not noticed her under the covers. The woman then introduced us to her daughter and her daughter's newborn baby girl.

Tears began to stream down my cheeks, and I tried to play it off and pretend I was celebrating the birth of her new baby. You know: tears of joy. The real reason for my tears was the pain I was feeling thinking about what kind of life this poor child was going to have. *What chance does she have to get out of her circumstances? This sucks.*

I walked over to our sweet hostess and laid a hand on her shoulder. "Can I pray for you?" I asked.

"Pray for me?" she said as she smiled sweetly.

"Yes," I said.

"I'd actually like to pray for you," she said.

"For me?" I said, bewildered. I was thinking, *Why would she want to pray for me?*

Before I could catch myself I said it: "Why?"

She smiled, not at all offended by my question, and said, "Because you have way more things to distract you from our God than I do."

I hit that clean dirt floor on my knees as if God Himself had pushed me to the ground.

"Please, please pray for me."

The woman laid her hands on my shoulders and begged God to not allow me to get distracted by the things of this world. It truly is one of the best prayers anyone has ever spoken over me.

It was as if the Lord were saying, *"Shelene, that little baby belongs to me. That baby will be just fine. There's only one thing that baby needs to get right."*

There is only *one* thing we all need to get right, and that is to know and follow hard after Christ. God is at work all around us. We don't need to leave the country to see His hand at work. We just need to open our eyes and be willing to jump in.

Lord, help me fix my eyes on You and flee from the sin that can trip me up in my pursuit of a life that pleases You. Help me not be distracted by things that won't matter in a hundred years, and give me the energy to focus on the things that will. Amen.

NINETEEN

Kitchen Impossible

It was a hot, humid Caribbean morning already, and it was only nine o'clock. Our group of thirteen travelers had piled into a small white-and-blue bus, which began slowly working its way through the substantial single-lane morning traffic, with black smoke pouring out the back. Our translator, Jean-Pierre, had found the click button microphone, and with a considerable amount of static began to share that we were headed to a school in Caballona, Dominican Republic. He explained how Skip1 had provided the food, and our group would be serving the very first school lunch these children had ever had in the three and a half years since the school had opened.

As we pulled up to the tin-roofed, light-blue-painted block school building, we saw a large group of kids waiting for us on an uneven, cracked basketball court with rusty, slightly bent, no-net baskets. Bits of windblown trash spotted the dirt schoolyard.

The director greeted us with an enthusiastic smile, and she and Jean-Pierre began to give us a tour of the humble facility. As we walked into the different classrooms, we noticed large vertical shutters on the open-air windows (no glass) that provided ventilation from the afternoon Caribbean breezes. In the midst of our tour, our host walked us past an open section of dirt on the property and I asked the director, "What is your dream for this piece of land?"

Without hesitation she said, "To build a kitchen. I'd like a kitchen so that the children can have lunch every day. Some of the kids are so hungry they can't even concentrate to read the chalkboard. If we had a kitchen I could at least make sure they received one meal a day."

"Well, how much is a kitchen?"

"It's very costly," she said.

"It's okay. How much?"

"Probably about twelve thousand US dollars."

"I think we might be able to help you with that."

I am convinced God has a majestic-sized sense of humor. The sheer fact that God would have Skip1 building kitchens still cracks up my husband and me to this very day. You see, I am anything but a good cook. In fact, cooking is quite high on my list of most-hated activities, and I barely use my own kitchen. Visitors to my house often notice a plaque hanging over my stovetop. It was a gift from a dear friend who knows me well. It reads, "Guess what I made for dinner? Reservations." No joke.

As our team started serving lunch to the schoolchildren, I couldn't help but notice children peering longingly through openings in the fence. Some of the schoolchildren started taking plates and handing them to the children standing outside the fenced-in area. These were hungry children who weren't fortunate enough to attend the school. "Is it possible to open the gates and feed as many children as we can?" I asked Jean-Pierre and the school director.

They assessed the amount of food available and said yes. We opened the gates and let them in to enjoy lunch as well.

Some in our group began a basketball game, which needed no translator. That day in Caballona, we didn't care where these kids were from, and the kids didn't care where we were from. They were present enough in the moment to love on each other with their time and full attention.

As our team set out to visit Haiti in the morning, the possibility of building a kitchen at the school was the main topic of conversation. We started brainstorming about setting up a spot on our website where everyone back home in America could skip one lunch, and those funds would go specifically to this project so these kids could have lunch every day. *If everyone skipped with this goal in mind,* I thought, *we could raise the funds to build this kitchen in no time.* Over the next two days, I was focused on and obsessed with getting all the necessary information, dimensions, specifications, and contractor leads.

A few days later, we boarded the plane to head back to the United States. I couldn't wait to share with the Skip1 board and team about the kitchen opportunity we had stumbled upon. But I felt a little like I had missed out on the people I had come to meet and touch. Instead of meeting with those kids reaching through the fence, I had been busy worrying about measuring out the length of the kitchen.

Sometimes we get so focused on the *doing* that we fail to

embrace the *being*. Love skips the comforts and jumps right into the action of meeting people where they are, and sometimes that's on the basketball court; sometimes it's sitting in a single-room house with dirt floors and just talking with somebody in need.

I often think how many people God has had brush up against my life to possibly add an epic scene to my journey here on earth. Instead of stopping to check it out or, as our team members demonstrated, stopping to have a basketball game, I am too often guilty of making the project—not the people— the focus.

When I got back, I spent some time reflecting on how I had taken my focus off people on that trip. I was reminded of two sisters whose story is carefully recorded in the Bible. Luke 10:38–42 tells the story:

> As Jesus and his disciples were on their way, he came to a village where a woman named Martha opened her home to him. She had a sister called Mary, who sat at the Lord's feet listening to what he said. But Martha was distracted by all the preparations that had to be made. She came to him and asked, "Lord, don't you care that my sister has left me to do the work by myself? Tell her to help me!"
>
> "Martha, Martha," the Lord answered, "you are worried and upset about many things, but few things are needed—or indeed only one. Mary has chosen what is better, and it will not be taken away from her."

When I first read this story, I was incredulous. I thought Jesus got it all wrong. It was clear to me that Mary was a suck-up, a lazy dog, a teacher's pet. On the other hand, Martha's the mover and shaker. We should call her the first Martha Stewart. She can multitask and do it all well, with style. Martha was literally doing it all: throwing a party, keeping her house clean, preparing the food for Jesus and His disciples. Mary, on the other hand, was completely clueless to her sister's smoke signals and fireworks show.

"Yo, Mary!" I can just see Martha tapping her foot and waving her dish towel. *"Hello?* Can I get a little help here?"

Mary was completely oblivious to her big sister. She was in a place not even meant for her. In those days women didn't commonly hang out with men. In the culture of the time, a woman's place was in the kitchen. Nevertheless, there Mary sat, focused on one thing: Jesus.

Frustrated, Martha finally burst into the man meeting to point out that Mary had been slacking. Jesus would surely order Mary out at once to help her sister with the meal, Martha thought. But to Martha's astonishment, Jesus had a different view. He said, "Mary has chosen what is better, and it will not be taken away from her."

See how wrong our perspective can be? The Bible says Jesus called out Martha, saying, "You are worried and upset about many things." Sound like anyone you know . . . maybe personally? Maybe *you*? It sure sounds a lot like me at times, worried and upset about many things, but few things are needed.

I get distracted, sometimes with good things. Even in the midst of a mission trip, I can get distracted. Much like Martha, instead of sitting at Jesus' feet, I am too often focused on tending to the kitchen. Just like Mary, I have learned God is far more concerned with my full attention on Him than He is interested in me getting a job done for Him.

The Bible says man looks at the outward appearance, but God looks at the heart (1 Samuel 16:7). God is not looking at our social, work, athletic, or color-coded kids calendar. He's not concerned or stressed over who's set to host Thanksgiving this year or who's cooking Christmas dinner. The Lord commands us in Psalms, "Be still, and know that I am God" (46:10).

I am such a Martha that my friend Laurie actually painted this verse over my bathtub. *Be still, Shelene, and know that I am God!* I'm the girl who wants so badly to have Mary moments with God that I schedule them and fail, instead of just being ever present in the awe and wonder He's creating all around me.

Has your focus on a task ever gotten in the way of people? I remember a time I was working on preparing for a meeting at my house for some Skip1 donors. With fewer than forty minutes until my guests were going to arrive, I still needed to pick up the hors d'oeuvres and fruit platter for the meeting. I jumped into my SUV and rushed to the Whole Foods Market near my house.

Pulling into the parking lot, I spied a rare front-row parking space. I jammed my foot to the accelerator, and my big SUV rocketed into it. Stopping with a screech, I looked over and realized that in my big hurry I had blatantly cut off a little convertible Fiat whose owner had wisely chosen not to play chicken with the crazy lady in the SUV four times its size. As I looked closer at the red convertible I had cut off, I was mortified to see that it looked like an eighty-year-old woman was driving. Ashamed at my impatience, I got out of my car and waited for the sweet old lady to park a few rows down and get out of her car.

As she exited her car, I ran up and said, "I am so sorry. Please forgive me for my impatience and laziness in taking that closer parking spot from you."

"No problem, honey," she said in a crisp, cheerful voice. "I just came from my Zumba class at the gym, and I'm always up for burning a few extra calories."

Ugh. Double guilt, first for my impatience and second for my laziness.

It is in those moments, when we are so focused on the task, that we fail to see God or the people around us. He puts them in our path, and we miss it. For Jesus, the person standing in front of Him was His ministry. Many times we see the person standing in front of us as an obstacle.

God still loves the Marthas and the type A personalities of the world. He purposefully made each of us unique and in His image. In the body of Christ, both Marys and Marthas are needed. Just don't miss Jesus and what He has for you in the scheduling and task execution of life. As Christians, we can actually complete an assignment but never experience God. He is far more interested in us walking with Him than He is in us getting a job done for Him.

Lord, help me recognize the opportunities for ministry You have put in my path. But in my quest to serve You and others, don't let me forget to see the people who need You. Help me not worry about things that really don't matter but, instead, choose what is better: knowing and loving You. Amen.

TWENTY

Full Circle: Skip1 Night

The Skip1 board had been floating the concept of a fund-raiser dinner for years. They wanted our team to share with our faithful donors all that Skip1.org has been doing around the world. I was always reluctant. Understand, I love a good party like the next girl, but to be honest, I've been to lots of fund-raiser dinners for charities, and I have mixed feelings about them.

I actually like them: interesting people, amazing venues, and as a rule, always great food. The thing that bugged me was that on the way home after each event, I was always adding up costs in my head. After getting a headache from number crunching, I would inevitably say to Brice, "I sure hope they raised enough money to cover their costs."

So whenever the fund-raiser dinner idea came up with the Skip1 board, I expressed my reservations. Finally, they got serious and brought it up again, and we all decided to pray on it and circle back around the next month. As I prayed, I got a clear idea for how our first ever Skip1 fund-raiser gala should look. The more I thought about it, the more excited I got. The night before the board meeting, I was having trouble getting to sleep.

The next day when the meeting opened, I said, "I know for

years I have been very reluctant to do a fund-raising dinner. I just hate to spend money feeding people who really don't need to be fed. But as some of you know, I have had an idea that would allow me to embrace a fund-raiser dinner. We just need to skip all the normal things that happen at fund-raiser dinners."

I looked across the room, and some faces were a bit confused. "Like what?" somebody asked.

"Like the dinner. I'm not kidding. What if we could have people pay the ticket price for a swanky dinner, and not feed them? We could raise enough money in one sitting to build the kitchen in Rwanda we have wanted to build."

I went on to explain how I wanted to skip all the fluff. Skip the raffle prizes, the silent auctions, the stuff that people bid on. Everybody loved the skipping idea and we decided that if anyone got really upset that he or she was not served dinner, we would just give that individual's money back, along with a gift certificate to McDonald's.

Then I said, "I know what I'm about to say is impossible, and that's why I love it. You all know how I've shared my story since 2003 about visiting my sponsored child in Uganda. Well, I'd like to fly Omega out here to America and surprise everyone at the event."

The board members all loved it.

Matt Warren and Drew Lucas are the magic behind Radar Creative and are Skip1 board members extraordinaire. They took the lead and secured an amazing venue at the oldest studio in Hollywood, the old Warner studio now called "The Lot."

Matt set up a lunch meeting with the owner and chef of Global Cuisine, Gary Arabia. Gary runs Sound Stage 7 at the Lot and is well known in entertainment circles for catering fabulously glamorous events for the Oscars, Grammys, and Golden Globes, just to name a few.

At lunch I shared my story with Gary. Then I shared my desire to have ninety fake servers walk out in black pants and white shirts, looking sharp, each with two plates of food covered with shiny metal covers. The covered plates would be set in front of the guests. In unison, the fake waiters would lift the lids to reveal completely empty plates. Imprinted on each plate would be a picture of one of the many children we serve. The amount of money raised from the dinner ticket sales—like, twenty thousand dollars—would flash on the screens. Then I would say from the stage, "Well, everyone, we just skipped dinner and raised twenty thousand dollars—enough to build the kitchen in Rwanda."

As I finished explaining our proposed night, I looked at Gary and thought he was going to burst out crying. He said, "Shelene, I've run this stage for years and have thrown some huge parties, from A-list actors to wonderful charitable events, but I have never heard of someone wanting to do what you're going to do."

Then this man, whom I had met only minutes earlier, added, "I'd like to provide the food for your event. I don't want your guests going home hungry. I will cover the cost. After the reveal of the empty plates, we will invite them out to the patio for an hors d'oeuvres dinner."

"What? Are you kidding me?" Thank you, Gary-I-just-met-you-Arabia.

He then set up a day and time for our team to visit his restaurant for a sampling of the yummy gourmet foods he'd be preparing.

The venue was shaping up, but one thing was not. Getting a fourteen-year-old girl named Omega a visa to leave Uganda and visit America was one tall order. Apparently, due to the serious concern that young people would never be willing to leave the United States once they arrive, getting a visa for Omega in the time frames we needed was nearly impossible.

By now I think you know how I deal with impossible situations. I jump all in.

I just kept praying, trusting what I felt the Lord was telling me.

Barbara and I Skyped with people we had relationships with on the ground in Gaba, Uganda. They got Omega her passport, but when I started talking about getting Omega's visa, everybody laughed and smiled and told us not to get our hopes up. "Deez tings are not eezy," we were told.

My hopes were plenty high, yet I had peace either way.

Then reservations began to creep into my mind about Omega coming. *Shelene, the last time you saw Omega in person was six years ago*, I thought. *What if she's shy, like most of the kids? What if she freaks out in front of an audience? What if she freezes up on the stage, under the lights, with hundreds of people staring at her? Perhaps it would be best to send a film crew to shoot a video of her, where she lives, her school, and call it a day. That way you can have several takes. If the video does not come out, you don't have to use it.*

At one point, when the event was just two months away with

still no answers about the visa, I had friends ask, "Shelene, what's your plan B?" I kept praying for a plan B, but only plan A stayed on my heart: skip the food and bring Omega here to the United States.

Then we got news that Omega had an appointment set up at the US embassy.

Several days before Omega's appointment, her mom was talking to her boss at the hotel where she worked. She told him that Omega had the opportunity to possibly come to the United States, she had her airline ticket and her passport, and she was praying to God to allow the customs officials to approve her visa.

"Well, let me tell you," the man said, "I have been applying for a visa to visit the US year after year for over six years. I am a well-established business owner with a family and money in the bank to come back to, yet I have been denied time and time again. I have yet to receive a visa. Do not be disappointed if you do not get a visa for your daughter."

Finally, the day came for Omega to go to the embassy. There she would meet with customs officials who would decide if she was going to get the visa. Omega's mom; her proposed chaperone for the trip, Edith; and Kenneth, a social worker from ARM (the ministry in Gaba), all went with Omega.

At the appointed time, a stern-looking female customs official took Omega and her mom back into a bare room that contained only one metal desk and two chairs. "Please have a seat."

Omega and her mother slid into the two metal chairs in front of the customs officer's desk. The officer examined Omega's papers with a severe scowl.

"What's your name?"

"Omega."

"Your full name," the officer said with a harsh look of impatience.

"Omega Veronica Nabisere."

"Is this your mom?"

"Yes."

"Why do you want to go to the United States?"

"To visit my sponsor."

"Is your mom okay with that?" said the officer, nodding toward Omega's mom.

"Oh yes, very happy with that."

"What are you planning to do while you are there?"

"I will visit my sponsor and attend the Skip1 Night gala event to raise money for my village. We have a letter from Skip1 explaining the event." The officer eyed the paper skeptically, then took it and read the short paragraphs explaining the gala.

"Do you have a dad?"

"No, he died when I was very young."

"Why does your sponsor want you to come to America?"

"To attend the Skip1 gala."

"Is your dad okay with it?"

"My dad's dead."

After several more questions that seemed to peculiarly repeat, the seemingly grouchy customs official hustled out.

A few minutes later, Edith, Omega's chaperone, who had been taken into a similar room, received a visit from the same stern-faced official. The official asked her similarly repetitive questions. Apparently the repeated questions are US Customs' effort to test the stories to see if they would remain consistent.

Later, as Omega was telling me this story, she said, "Mamma Shelene, nobody from my school had ever been in the US embassy. When you are in the embassy, you are already in America. I felt so blessed just to be in the US embassy, so no matter what happened with the visa, I told God I was fine with it."

After what seemed like a long time, the scowling woman reappeared, somehow looking less severe. "Well, Omega," she announced, "you had better plan to come back tomorrow."

"Come back tomorrow? Okay. But why?"

"Well, you want to pick up your visa, don't you?" The scowl that had seemed to be etched in stone was now replaced by a big smile.

Omega, unable to contain her excitement, jumped into the air with a bounce and shouted, "Thank you! Thank you so much! Thank you so much!"

The impossible had happened. Omega was coming to America. When word reached us back in the states, we all celebrated.

Meanwhile, Omega's mom couldn't wait to tell her boss. The next time she worked, she told him, "God has given Omega a visa." When he expressed his surprise, she responded, "It was God. Sir, you just need to repent and get saved."

The long-awaited day finally arrived. All the preparations had been made, and Skip1 Night was finally here.

The guests began to arrive at the Lot. Instead of a red carpet, the guests walked down the green carpet to get pictures with friends and family and then enter Sound Stage 7. Since the night was all about raising funds for a kitchen we wanted to build in Africa, after stepping off the green carpet, to enter Stage 7 the guests had to walk through a re-created third-world kitchen.

Sean and Cheril Hendry had used a photograph of a dilapidated kitchen that Cheril had taken on our trip to Haiti and duplicated it. There was an open cooking fire, hubcaps for pot holders, a dirt floor, and wooden sticks for utensils. Gentlemen in their fine loafers and ladies looking glamorous in high heels all got to tromp across the dirt floor of this reconstructed kitchen as a reminder of the looming needs across the world.

The sound stage had been entirely whited out—even the floor had been painted white. The colored lighting made the place feel glamorously bright. The focal point of the room over the stage was projected with the now-familiar green Skip1 logo.

The tables had been beautifully set with wine glasses, water goblets, salad plates, linen napkins, and silverware. No detail was forgotten. The setting wowed everyone, and it looked as though we were all about to enjoy an amazing feast.

I opened the night with a welcome and a few quick remarks about the mission of Skip1: to skip something and donate the value of that item to bring food to a needy family. Then I said, "With no further ado, it's time to eat."

Instantly, ninety waiters entered the room, carrying the covered "entrées." They placed the covered plates in front of our two hundred dinner guests.

"Bon appétit!" I said.

All at once, in a single motion, the waiters lifted the covers to reveal empty plates. The dinner guests were stunned. Then suddenly they erupted in applause all around the room, and people began standing to their feet. I grabbed the microphone.

"I've wanted to say this for months," I began. "We skipped dinner, and as a result actually raised enough money to build an entire kitchen at a school in Rwanda to feed kids every day." The number $20,194, measuring fifteen feet tall, flashed in green on each side of the stage. "Please take a look at that number. By skipping dinner you have really made a difference tonight."

Then I said, "I want to introduce you all to Chef Gary Arabia."

Gary walked out onstage.

"Gary did not want any of you upset with me or to go home hungry tonight," I went on, "so he prepared a little gourmet treat for you all. Now we would like to invite you to go out to the patio, where Mr. Arabia and his staff will serve a donated appetizer dinner."

The party moved out to the patio, and the guests enjoyed delectable seared scallops with curried polenta, short ribs of beef with a port wine glaze, pearl pasta tossed with Japanese eggplant and chanterelle mushrooms, and pan-seared sea bass with a miso glaze. Needless to say, nobody went away hungry.

After dinner, the crowd made their way back into Sound Stage 7, where Drew, from the singing talent show *The X Factor*, entertained us with a song she had written.

Afterward, I took the stage and reminded our guests how Skip1 started and how meeting my sponsored little girl, Omega, when she was four years old had changed her life and mine forever. "I wish I could take all of you to Uganda with me to meet Omega and see her mud hut and visit her school," I told them, "but obviously I can't."

The audience seemed to empathize, as if they really all wanted to go experience what I had experienced.

I continued, "So instead of taking you all with me, tonight we brought Omega here to meet you. Omega, please come out and meet my friends."

With that, the now-teenage Omega, decked out in quite possibly the most glamorous dress of the night, walked onstage. Once again the audience was on their feet.

What happened next was beyond anything I could have hoped or imagined.

Omega took the microphone from me and, without notes, spoke from her heart. For twenty minutes she shared her love for her country and about this once-in-a-lifetime opportunity she was having, coming to America and meeting her brother Blake, her sister Brooke, but most importantly her dad Brice.

She next related how she remembered getting her picture taken by ARM (African Renewal Ministries) in Uganda when she was four, how she had prayed and asked God to give her a sponsor, and how sheer joy had come over her when she found out the Lord provided one. Not one of her friends had ever met their sponsors, she told the Skip1 audience, so when word spread to her village that her sponsor was in Gaba, she could hardly believe it. But it was true. She had instantly become a celebrity in her village.

"My sponsor returned again, and then a third time, and then I never saw her again," she shared, winking at me as I stood onstage. "Until now."

I've heard the saying that things come full circle. Now I was experiencing it firsthand.

As Omega continued to speak to the crowded room, you could have heard a pin drop. She told them about her first plane ride. "I could have lived on the plane," she said. "I had a nice seat, a TV, a toilet, and they even had food on the plane. The food was too spicy for me, but still, I was thankful. I felt a little dizzy when the plane lifted off the ground. I had only seen planes in the air, so I could not believe how big it was and how many people could fit on it.

"Partway through the thirteen-hour flight, I had to use the toilet. When I pushed the flush button, it almost sucked me down the hole. I ran out of the bathroom so fast the nice flight attendant had to assure me I'd be okay and sent me back in to finish my duties.

"When I got to my sponsor's house, I had my own room, with a bed and a bathroom. I took my first shower, which was awesome. At home I bathe in a washbasin and splash the water over my head, but here in America, it's like I'm standing in the rain."

When Omega had first arrived at our house, I'd instructed her to get cleaned up by taking a shower. When she finished her shower, I went into her room to tell her we'd be leaving for dinner soon. She was scrubbing something out in the sink.

Omega looked at me, pointed to the shower, and said, "Does this warm water work in there?"

"Yes, of course," I said. "Omega, what are you doing, honey?"

"Oh, Mum," she said, "I am washing out my knickers."

"Your knickers?"

I walked over to the sink to see the bowl full of sudsy water and her underwear soaking in the bubbles. Seeing how it was her only pair, she was used to washing them out every night so that they'd be ready in the morning. My mind was spinning. Humbled, I asked, "Omega, did you take a cold shower?"

"Yes," she said, smiling. "I didn't want to bother you or make you have to boil the water for a hot bath."

"Yeah, about that . . . come here, honey." I walked her over to the shower and pointed to *H* and *C* on the faucet dial. "*H* is for hot. *C* for cold. Just turn the handle to the exact temperature you'd like."

"*Wow*, Mum. That's amazing," she said.

"Also, Omega, we have a washing machine. When your clothes need cleaning, you don't need to wash them out in the sink. Just give them to me, and I'll load them into the machine to clean them real good for you."

"Wow, Mum! That's wonderful."

At that instant I glanced over to see Blake and Brooke standing in the doorway to Omega's room. They had just heard Omega's statement of joy over a machine that had caused many arguments in our home. That joy over the washing machine hit them hard in their hearts. Never again would they complain when I asked them to throw a load of laundry in to be washed or to fold a load of laundry out of the dryer. Those are what I like to call *first-world problems*.

Blake and Brooke were in awe watching Omega's reaction to many firsts. Her first piece of pizza (which, surprisingly, she did not like), her first Starbucks, her first visit to their school. But back to the dinner . . .

Next, Omega shared with the guests that after the event tonight, she was going to Disneyland! "My friends at home will never believe me. They are already saying, 'Omega, you say you're a Christian. Why do you lie? How can you be in Hollywood and at Disneyland the next day?'

"My friends back home think Hollywood is a studio where they make movies. They are never going to believe me that it's a city and Disneyland is not just a place where they make cartoons, but it's a place for fun.

"All of these things I've seen and done have been awesome, but I must say, the best thing about this trip to America is meeting my dad Brice."

Omega had lost her dad when she was very young, so to have the love of a father like Brice these past two weeks had changed her life. "Since I have been here, every morning my dad Brice has said, 'Good morning, Omega. How did you sleep?' I have never had someone do that. Then he'd say, 'Omega, what would you like for breakfast, honey?' Nobody has ever asked me what I like. Where I come from, you get what they give you, and that's what you like."

By this time there wasn't a dry eye in Studio 7. I took the microphone back from Omega.

"And I was afraid you weren't going to talk."

The audience roared with laughter.

Continuing, I said, "Omega, we have a surprise for you."

Our Skip1 friend, award-winning actor and director Cole Hauser, stepped onto the stage.

"Omega," he began, "as I sat in the audience with my nine-year-old son, Ryland, I could not help but think . . ." Then he looked at me. "Shelene, I think you've met your match. If I didn't know better, I'd have thought you gave birth to this child yourself."

Laughs and applause erupted from the crowd.

"Omega," he went on, "on behalf of Skip1, we would like to

present you with a check for five thousand dollars for your college education in Uganda, where we believe you are going to be a world changer. Everyone here can attest that you have already changed our world tonight."

These are the moments movies are made of. As guests rose to their feet, Omega hugged Cole, and she exited the stage. Soon, lines of people were waiting to meet her and get a picture with her. It was a really good night. A journey that had begun with one simple, sincere *yes* ten years earlier for me had come full circle, and, indeed, everything in my life had been changed.

Here I was, looking at a young lady who quite possibly could have been dead if it had not been for my intervention. Instead, this beautiful young girl was using her voice to tell her story and to encourage the people in this room to make a difference in somebody's life. Her joyful smile and excitement had just ignited and energized an entire sound stage full of people.

As I thought about the kitchens we had built, the countless meals that had been served, and kids who had been spared the agony of starvation, I lifted my head toward heaven, stared high up into the rafters of a one-hundred-year-old sound stage, and whispered up a thank-you to God for just letting me be a small part of this picture. I had never dreamed that one small *yes* would so significantly touch the lives of so many people.

At that moment, I realized I had learned a valuable lesson. It is in sacrificially loving others that God can use us and fulfill us in a way that nothing else can. By surrendering our plans and desires to Him, we can be a part of something He wants to do.

I dare you to say yes to God and watch Him take you on an adventure of a lifetime.

Lord, help me remember that I need to make myself available for Your plans. Saying yes to Your plans can change my life and result in great joy. Help me understand that every single person counts and every action I take can affect somebody's life for the good or the bad. Give me the courage to trust in Your power to do what You want, even against impossible odds. Amen.

Conclusion

Coming to the concluding section of a book all about loving, skipping, and jumping, you can probably guess the question I am about to ask.

Are you ready to jump?

Jumping is all about taking action. For some of you, you know exactly what you are called to do. If that's you, now is the time to resolve to do it. It is time to get your feet moving. I suggest you stop reading right now and start putting the jump ball in action. Yes, put this book down now and make your first step, jump, or quantum leap. This book will still be here for you in a few minutes, hours, or days after you take your first steps.

Perhaps you are someone who at this moment does not yet know what your jump is going to be. You may be wondering what in the world God wants you to do. You would do it if you knew, but you just aren't sure what your jump should look like.

Maybe you are supposed to travel with Skip1.org and me to Africa or South America to help feed children who are in need. God might be challenging you to sell some of that excess stuff in your life that you really don't need and donate the proceeds of that car, motor home, cabin, boat, bicycle, or whatever, to save the lives of hundreds of children just like the little seven-year-old boy I met in Fishers Village.

It's possible you have loathed the sight of homeless people, as I did, and God wants you to go help the "least of these" on the street corner in your own neighborhood. Perhaps God wants you to downsize your house and use the excess money to help others.

I have noticed that many times in my life I have had a moment of epiphany but let that crucial moment of decision pass without taking action. That is typical for many people who are on the verge of a decision that will change everything, and yet they put off making the hard decisions. After reading the examples and stories in this book, you have seen I have absolutely no regrets for the time and resources I have expended in caring for the "least of these." Do not let this moment pass without committing to working out your *jump*.

A LIFE OF LOVE, SKIP, AND JUMP

One of the most shining examples of the concept of Love, Skip, Jump is a man born more than two hundred years ago. I am talking about the nineteenth-century pastor George Müller (1805–1898). Müller was an amazing man who, though born in Germany, spent most of his life in England, pastoring his church for sixty-six years (1830–1898). Müller passionately loved God.

He created five separate ministries while still pastoring, including (1) schools for children and adults; (2) Bible distribution; (3) missionary support; (4) tract and book printing and distribution; and (5) boarding, clothing, and educating orphans. As part of his orphan work, he built five orphanages, which by the end of his life held two thousand orphans at any given time. In his lifetime he was personally responsible for caring for 10,024 orphans. This was a man who knew how to *love*.

In October 1830, Müller gave up his regular salary from his church. Throughout his entire ministry he refused to directly ask anyone for money to support the orphans or himself. He never took out a loan and was never in debt. When he had a financial crisis and no money to buy food for the orphans, he was heard to say, "How the means are to come, I know not, but I know that God is almighty and that He hears, and the hearts of all are in His hands. If He pleases to influence persons, they will help."

This is a man who was willing to *skip* and would trust God to provide.

Here is what I found most amazing about George Müller's life: beginning at age seventy, he spent the next seventeen years, until he was eighty-seven, traveling to forty-two different countries and preaching an average of seven times per week. This was a man who knew how to *jump*.

George Müller had a method by which he would test to see what God wanted him to do. I have personally used his method, which I've summarized below, to help me seek what God has wanted me to do in countless situations. The quotes under each point are from Müller.[1]

1. GET YOUR WILL OUT OF THE WAY.

"I seek at the beginning to get my heart into such a state that it has no will of its own in regard to a given matter."

This is the rather difficult act of trying to take my human desires out of the way.

2. AVOID FEELINGS AND IMPRESSIONS. THEY CAN LEAD TO DELUSIONS.

"Having done this, I do not leave the result to feeling or simple impression. If so, I make myself liable to great delusions."

3. SEEK THE WILL OF THE SPIRIT IN CONNECTION WITH THE WORD.

"I seek the will of the Spirit of God through, or in connection with, the Word of God. The Spirit and the Word must be combined. If I look to the Spirit alone without the Word, I lay myself open to great delusions also. If the Holy Ghost guides us at all, He will do it according to the Scriptures and never contrary to them."

4. CONSIDER PROVIDENTIAL CIRCUMSTANCES.

"Next, I take into account providential circumstances. These often plainly indicate God's will in connection with His Word and Spirit."

Sometimes God can bring about or allow happenings in your life that will circumstantially open or close doors, for example, a delayed or missed flight that closes a prospect, an unexpected bonus that opens an opportunity you had been praying about, or a seemingly coincidental encounter that opens up a new relationship.

5. PRAY.

"I ask God in prayer to reveal His will to me aright."

6. MAKE A DELIBERATE JUDGMENT, AND THEN KEEP TESTING IT WITH PRAYER.

"Thus, through prayer to God, the study of the Word, and reflection, I come to a deliberate judgment according to the best of my ability and knowledge; and if my mind is thus at peace, and continues so after two or three more petitions, I proceed accordingly. In trivial matters, and in transactions involving the most important issues, I have found this method always effective."

I challenge you to use this method to help you work out your Love, Skip, Jump opportunities. I think you will find that seeking God's wisdom for your life in such a complete way will help you make choices that will fit into a two-hundred-year plan for your life.

———

This book opened with a description of one of my favorite scenes from *Willy Wonka & the Chocolate Factory*. When Veruca Salt mocked Wonka's lickable schnozberries, she sealed her own fate. Unfortunately, Veruca missed out on the opportunity of a lifetime.

But the story does not end there.

With all the children gone but one, Charlie gets called on the carpet for stealing a Fizzy Lifting Drink. Though Charlie was promised a "lifetime supply of chocolate," Mr. Wonka angrily tells Grandpa Joe that because Charlie broke the rules, he will get nothing. Furious, Grandpa Joe advises, "Come on, Charlie. . . . If Slugworth wants a Gobstopper, he'll get one." Earlier, Mr. Slugworth, Wonka's conniving rival, had offered Charlie enough money to take care of his poor mom and grandparents for the rest of their lives—if he would bring him a single piece of candy from Wonka's factory, specifically, an Everlasting Gobstopper.

But as Charlie is about to walk out the door with his Gobstopper, which Wonka had given him with the condition that he *solemnly swear* to keep it to himself, he stops. His conscience won't allow him to betray the trust Mr. Wonka had put in him. Charlie reaches his hand in his pocket and walks back over to the desk where Mr. Wonka is busily working. He places the Everlasting Gobstopper in front of Mr. Wonka and turns to leave.

Suddenly Mr. Wonka jumps up. "Charlie . . . You did it! . . . You passed the test."

You see, "Slugworth" wasn't really Slugworth at all, but Mr. Wilkinson, an employee of Wonka's whom he'd assigned to put Charlie to the test, to see if he would be true to his word or choose betrayal for the sake of instant riches.

Near the end of the movie, Mr. Wonka takes Charlie and Grandpa Joe to the Wonkavator—a glass elevator that can go "sideways and slantways and longways and backways and squareways and frontways and any other ways that you can think of," and the three get in. The elevator shoots out of the roof and over the city.

As they fly over London in the Wonkavator, Wonka asks, "How did you like the chocolate factory, Charlie?"

"I think it's the most wonderful place in the whole world."

"I'm very pleased to hear you say that because I'm giving it to you. That's all right, isn't it? I can't go on forever, and I don't really want to try. So, who can I trust to run the factory when I leave and take care of the Oompa Loompas for me? Not a grownup. A grownup would want to do everything his own way, not mine. That's why I decided a long time ago I had to find a child. A very honest, loving child to whom I can tell all my most precious candy making secrets."

"And that's why you sent out the golden tickets," Charlie says.

"That's right. So the factory's yours, Charlie. You can move in immediately."

"What happens to the rest of—" Charlie starts to ask, but Wonka answers before he can even finish his question.

"The whole family. I want you to bring them all."

The very thing Charlie thought he was giving up by giving back the Everlasting Gobstopper—wealth and security for his family—had become his. By doing what he knew was right, he gained everything and the adventure of a lifetime. You can too.

You may think that by loving, skipping, and jumping you are giving up opportunity and prosperity for yourself or your family, but really the opposite is true. God's reality is a lot more like the Chocolate Factory than you might think.

Acknowledgments

TO BRICE:

The love of my life, my godly husband, and best friend. You are my James 1:19 man: quick to listen, slow to speak, slow to anger. Thank you for making me feel like I'm the only person in the room in your eyes. Thank you for your support, time, and sacrifice in making this book a reality. I love you.

TO MY SON, BLAKE:

You are a young man after God's own heart. Your sincere love for God and people humbles me every day. You fill our home with such joy. You have the gifts of wisdom, leadership, and service. Dad and I both know that God has *huge* adventures planned for your life. Keep loving Him most.

TO MY DAUGHTER, BROOKE:

Brookie Cookie Star, my little assistant. God has created you for such a time as now. Your kind, loving, servant's heart blesses me every day. I love watching you play lacrosse and the leadership, love, and integrity you bring to your team. You are a world changer and a young woman of your word. I love you with all my heart. Keep saying *yes* to God.

TO SHANDA WEAVER:

The best little sister on the planet, my "brother-in-love" Greg, and my two beautiful nieces, Madison and Saige. Thank you for taking many of these crazy adventures with me. Always willing to serve. Always willing to put God first. I am blessed God gave me all of you. I love you with all my heart.

TO BARBARA CAMERON:

Buddy!! What can I say—you have been my mentor since I was twenty-two. We have traveled the world together. Grown in our walks with the Lord. Shared the ups and downs, always knowing who was in complete control. Your loyalty, love, and friendship have blessed me more than words can say.

TO POPS:

Pops . . . I love you with all my heart and thank God for placing you in my life twenty-one years ago. I love our weekly Bible study lunches together. Watching you care for, love, and be devoted to Kay has made a huge impact in my marriage. You are a man of your word. In sickness and in health. I am so glad I get to spend eternity with you. Keep investing in the "First National Bank of Heaven." As it has been said, he is no fool who gives what he cannot keep to gain what he cannot lose.

TO KAY:

You are Marvelous! I can't read Hebrews 13:2 without thinking of you. (The verse that says you may be entertaining angels without knowing it.) You are one of God's angels in my life, reminding me that joy comes not from our circumstances but from the Lord. God has prepared a special place for you in heaven.

TO MY GIRLFRIENDS:

Proverbs 27:6: "Faithful are the wounds of a friend, wicked are the kisses of your enemies."

You are the women I call when I need biblical truth. You are my prayer warrior sisters, fellow followers of Jesus Christ. I thank God for allowing me not just to know you on earth but also to have the gift of spending eternity with you forever. I love you—Barbara Cameron, Lisa Chan, Candace Cameron Bure, Karen Russell, Deb Lautner, Michelle Hiepler, Cheril Hendry, Chelsea Cameron, Shannon McIntosh, Laurie Steinfeld, and Karen Armstrong.

TO FRANCIS AND LISA CHAN:

To the best pastor and pastor's wife on the planet. Your unfaltering commitment to teach the truth of God's Word even when it was hard has impacted my life more than you'll ever know. Your example of living and loving like Jesus is changing the world. Thank you both for loving me, my marriage, and my children and for sharing your precious family with ours. I love you, Rachel, Mercy, Elle, Zeke, and Claire.

TO MATT WARREN AND DREW LUCAS:

The brothers I always wished I had. Thank you for always taking my calls when I have a crazy idea. Skip1.org would not exist without you two. Designing, creating, directing, traveling, your passion for Christ shines bright in the universe. I am blessed to know you both and call you family. www.radarla.com

ACKNOWLEDGMENTS

TO SARA HICKS:

Sweet Sara, thank you for keeping me young. Your desire to fall deeper and deeper in love with Christ is beautiful. Keep seeking first His kingdom and His righteousness.

MICHAEL AND RITA WARREN:

Thank you, Michael, for taking some of these crazy adventures with me; and, Rita, for letting him go. You two are a perfect example of a couple finishing well.

TO MY AGENT, RICK CHRISTIAN:

When I met you, Rick, on the set of Karen's movie, you told me I was going to write a book one day. You also told me that you'd be my agent. I thought you were crazy, but you were right on both accounts. Thanks to you and Debbie for holding my hand every step of the way. I am forever grateful to you and your entire staff at Alive Communications.

TO BRYAN NORMAN:

Thank you! No one would be reading this book if it weren't for you. You are a genius. Thank you for dreaming, believing, creating, and, most important, jumping with me.

TO CHAD CANNON:

Thank you for your phone call, my friend. You saw this book from a mile away. #grateful

TO THE WHOLE PUBLISHING TEAM AT THOMAS NELSON—YOU ALL ROCK:

Brian, Chad, Kristen, Janene, Renée, Emily, and Katy.

ACKNOWLEDGMENTS

TO THE SKIP1.ORG BOARD AND VOLUNTEERS:

Thank you for allowing me time to write this book. Thank you for loving the children we serve. Thank you for your consistent service and for showing up and living the adventure of yes.

TO OMEGA:

Our beautiful daughter in Uganda. God knew exactly what He was doing when He gave us YOU more than ten years ago. It was a complete miracle that you were able to visit us in America this year. Keep your eyes fixed on Jesus and He will direct your path. God has given you the gift of communication and compassion. I can't wait to see how He uses your life for His glory. We love you.

TO MY FOREVER FRIENDS AND FAMILY, YOU KNOW WHO YOU ARE. I LOVE YOU.

Notes

INTRODUCTION

1. *Willy Wonka & the Chocolate Factory*, directed by Mel Stuart (1971).
2. You can watch this scene on YouTube at http://www.youtube.com/watch?v=1M0eMkcc91E.

CHAPTER 3 · MASSIVE GOD, EPIC LOVE

1. J. I. Packer, *Knowing God Devotional Journal: A One-Year Guide*, ed. Carol Nystrum (Downers Grove, IL: InterVarsity, 2004), 94.

CHAPTER 4 · YOU'VE GOT TO JUMP

1. John Ortberg, *If You Want to Walk on Water, You've Got to Get Out of the Boat* (Grand Rapids: Zondervan, 2001), 17.

CHAPTER 5 · STEP IT UP

1. Bob Goff, *Love Does: Discover a Secretly Incredible Life in an Ordinary World* (Nashville: Thomas Nelson, 2012), xvi.

CHAPTER 6 · IMPOSSIBLE LIVING

1. Paul Proctor, "The Purpose Driven Hostage," on the Forgotten Word Ministries website, March 26, 2005, cited from CNN's recording of the interview, http://www.forgottenword.org/hostage.html.

2. Rick Warren, *The Purpose Driven Life: What on Earth Am I Here For?* exp. ed. (Grand Rapids: Zondervan, 2012), 328.
3. CNN.com, March 15, 2005, transcript. CNN's Tony Harris, Drew Griffin, KC Wildmoon, Mike Ahlers, Matt Sloane, Kathleen Johnston, Jeanne Meserve, Susan Candiotti, Mike Heard, Kimberly Osias, and Mike Brooks contributed to the report.

CHAPTER 8 · EVERY JUMP RIPPLES
1. https://www.bookitprogram.com/redzone/read_do/Water/ADropofWater.ai.pdf.

CHAPTER 9 · THE FEAR FACTOR
1. Francis Chan, *Crazy Love: Overwhelmed by a Relentless God* (Colorado Springs: David C. Cook, 2013), 131.

CHAPTER 12 · LANDLORD FROM HEAVEN
1. Paraphrases of Matthew 6:3 and Matthew 6:5–6.

CHAPTER 14 · THE BANKRUPT RICH
1. Kevin Watkins, *Human Development Report 2006: Beyond Scarcity: Power, Poverty and the Global Water Crisis*, eds. Bruce Ross-Larson, Meta de Coquereaumont, and Christopher Trott (New York: Palgrave Macmillan, 2006), 2, http://hdr.undp.org/en/media/HDR06-complete.pdf.
2. The miniature earth project, www.miniature-earth.com.
3. Ibid.
4. Ibid.
5. Quote from "Global Crisis and Its Effects in the Developed and Emergent Countries," *Emerging Markets Journal*, 54. The miniature earth project, www.miniature-earth.com.
6. Randy Alcorn, *Money, Possessions, and Eternity*, rev. ed. (Carol Stream, IL: Tyndale House, 2003), 47.
7. Ibid., 45.

CHAPTER 15 · FOR SALE BY GOD

1. Randy Alcorn, *Money, Possessions, and Eternity*, rev. ed. (Carol Stream, IL: Tyndale House, 2003), 38.

CONCLUSION

1. *George Müeller: Man of Faith*, a reprint of *An Hour with George Müeller: The Man of Faith to Whom God Gave Millions*, ed., pamphlet.

About the Author

Shelene Bryan is the founder and executive director of Skip1.org, a charity dedicated to challenging ordinary people to skip one thing for the sake of someone in need and donate to provide food and clean water. Shelene is a former Hollywood producer whose life took a dramatic turn when she took an adventure to Africa. Out of that experience she became passionate about eliminating poverty. Shelene is an accomplished national speaker who now turns her extraordinary ability to challenge and inspire to the written word. Her inspirational stories and real-life experiences have captured the affections of audiences across America. Shelene resides in Southern California with her husband and two children.

skip1.org

skip something. feed a child.

Skip1.org is committed to bringing food and water to children and families in need. We do this by building new kitchens and renovating existing ones, financially supporting food distribution and feeding programs in places where kitchens can't be built and by supporting clean water and sustainable agricultural initiatives as needed.

Skip1.org currently has active projects in the Dominican Republic, Peru, Uganda, Rwanda, the Philippines, and North America.

Join Shelene Bryan, **Skip1.org**'s founder and author of *Love, Skip, Jump* in skipping something to help us feed children in need across the country and around the world.